D1265531

A MOVEMENT APPROACH TO GAMES FOR CHILDREN

A MOVEMENT APPROACH TO GAMES FOR CHILDREN

PETER H. WERNER, P.E.D.

Associate Professor,
University of South Carolina,
College of Health and Physical Education,
Columbia, South Carolina

with 71 *illustrations*

THE C. V. MOSBY COMPANY

ST. LOUIS • TORONTO • LONDON 1979

Printed in the United States of America

The C. V. Mosby Company
11830 Westline Industrial Drive, St. Louis, Missouri 63141

Library of Congress Cataloging in Publication Data

Werner, Peter H
A movement approach to games for children.

Bibliography: p.
Includes index.
1. Physical education for children. 2. Games.
3. Motor ability in children. I. Title.
GV443.W443 372.8'6 78-31387
ISBN 0-8016-5416-5

VT/M/M 9 8 7 6 5 4 3 2 1 02/D/273

Preface

According to Piaget,* the primary goals of education are to develop individuals who are creative and inventive and who are discoverers. This implies that we must educate today's children to become adults who are capable of doing new things and do not simply repeat what other generations have done. We need to develop minds that are critical and do not simply accept everything they are offered. In short, education should prepare children for change. Education should enable them to meet any circumstance with a fair chance of success.† Teachers should do their utmost to help children prepare for the world of the future, whether it be simply maneuvering along sidewalks that will be even more crowded than now, controlling one's body in a strange environment, or driving the future version of popular transportation. Belief in this philosophy, together with acceptance that each child's ability differs and that a child learns best through discovery and doing, requires that we look closely at the way we teach children. For purposes of this book, these attitudes force careful evaluation of the games teachers use for children.

In spite of the wealth of literature regarding games for children, there exists only a scant amount of information that gets to the heart of play development, stages of learning, and games in which children have an input regarding rules and strategies. Most existing textbooks include games for children that are categorized by line, circle, scatter, and relay formations in which the teachers have all the decision-making power. The games are predetermined by rules in which the teacher "commands" the children to participate. Such games involve large groups of children, long waiting lines for a turn, elimination of the unsuccessful, and heavy stress on winning. Most games are also chosen by teachers who lack concern about the cognitive development of children and the appropriateness of games to fit

*Piaget, J.: Science of education and the psychology of the child, translated from the French by Derek Coltman, New York, 1970, Orion Press, Inc.
†Menuhin, Y.: Theme and variations, New York, 1972, Stein & Day, Publishers.

the movement pattern or the social and emotional development of children.

Although games traditionally are approached in this manner, recent research indicates several facts that warrant a new approach to children's games. For example, children prefer to play in small groups. They are interested in making decisions pertaining to the technical aspects of the games they play. And, most often, children want to play games for fun, skill development, and participation rather than to win.

In addition, current literature points to the fact that there are basically two types of games formats—conventional and original. A conventional game is one in which the rules are predetermined. Examples are football, basketball, soccer, and other national games with rules and governing bodies. All the games of low organization are examples of conventional children's games: duck, duck, goose; crows and cranes; and red rover. Most traditional lead-up games to team sports are also conventional. Original games are those in which the rules are made up or modified by the participants prior to or during the process of play. Most recreative or "pickup" games of two versus two, three versus three, etc. can be classified as original because the game rules and scoring are modified by the available equipment, time, and space, as well as ability levels of the players. Conventional games were at one time original. They had to be invented and modified until they crystallized into their present form.

Where a teacher falls on the continuum of conventional-original games becomes a matter of philosophical approach. A recent book by Morris* takes the point of view that conventional games are modified to meet the needs of children. One takes a conventional game, analyzes its format, and makes changes or allows the children to make changes. As a result, there is movement along the continuum toward the original. After children gain some skill and can apply rules and strategies, however, games move back along the continuum toward the conventional games and team sports found at the middle school and high school. Thus the progression leads from the conventional, toward the original, and back toward the conventional.

If one were to consider the emotional, social, physical, and intellectual growth of children, it might make more sense to begin children's games at the original end of the continuum and make a gradual transition toward the conventional while placing a constant value on modification to meet the needs of the players. When children are learning about games during their years in the primary grades, it may be best to have them explore and solve problems regarding manipulative concept development. Later it may be wise to implement these manipulative concepts into game situations. Thus the progression leads from original games toward conventional game implementation.

---

*Morris, G. S. D.: How to change the games children play, Minneapolis, 1976, Burgess Publishing Co.

It is the purpose of this book to provide a framework from which teachers and parents can guide the game activities of children. It provides the framework or environment in which they learn to play and to design their own games according to the size of the play group, stage of play development, ability levels, and interests of the group. It is within this framework that children's games will become truly children's games—not games that adults decide can fit the children's needs and interests.

Peter H. Werner

Contents

CHAPTER ONE

Introduction

WHAT IS PLAY?

At the outset it seems necessary to establish a philosophy or approach toward play for children that will set the stage for the contents of this book on games. "Let's PLAY a GAME"—invariably, one word accompanies the other. What is "play"? Can you play without having a game? Can you have a game without playing?

Neuman defines play as any behavior in which the criteria of internal locus of control, internal reality, and intrinsic motivation exist. Each criterion can be clearly illustrated with reference to games. When are you at play in a game? When someone tells you what to do or when you have the freedom to choose from among variables related to game playing? For an activity to be play or a game, the *control*, or decision-making process, must be in the hands of the child, not the teacher. Any situation in which the teacher makes all the decisions with regard to game choice, teams, rules, scoring, and other variables in the game situation cannot truly be called play. The children are merely pawns in an environment controlled by an adult. Such activity is more drill or work oriented than truly play oriented. Thus, in approaching games with children, a serious look must be taken at the teaching methods used, each of which will be explained in detail in a later section of this chapter.

To put control into proper perspective, we must ask to what extent children are capable of making decisions about their games. It is like sending a young child into a candy store with a quarter. There are so many choices the child becomes confused and does not know what to buy. It is better to limit the child's choices to a few pieces and thereby make the selection easier. Likewise, a game situation should start with only a few choices and gradually progress to a situation in which the child can completely control the game environment. The point is, however, that even at beginning levels children should be given some choices in their play activities.

Play situations must also respect the concept of *internal reality.* This means that the reality of life and concern for survival must be suspended and replaced by fantasy, make-believe, pretending, or role playing. Thus, in guiding the games of children, we must allow the reality of life to be suspended. Games that permit rules, procedures, and contents of play to be determined according to the child's wishes ensure internal reality.

In addition to locus of control and internal reality, a third determinant of play behavior is that the child must be *intrinsically motivated* to play a game. This means that motivation to play a game must come from within the child. Although motivational forces can stem from a variety of factors, it is more advantageous to have children participate in games through self-motivation, rather than through pressure from parents, teachers, peers, or any of a variety of socioeconomic factors. Games that teachers choose and direct often motivate some of the children. But those for whom the game is too easy or too difficult are often not motivated to fully participate. Therefore we should encourage children to develop games of their own design—games in which they are intrinsically motivated to play according to their ability levels and interests.

Some define play by its content or the behavior exhibited by people at play, but other researchers define play by its motive (Ellis). Play is said to be motivated by a need for meaningful stimulation or optimal arousal. The more novel, challenging, complex, and dissonant the activity, the more arousing and fulfilling it becomes. Work behavior is far more predictable than play behavior and, as a result, deals more in knowns than in unknowns. If we expect children to learn to deal with the unknown or unexpected, we should foster problem-solving behaviors in their play.

To answer the remaining questions first posed, we must consider the relationship between play and games. You can play without having a game, as in cognitive, verbal, social, imaginative, and fantasy play. You can dance as you play or do gymnastics, but you cannot truly engage in a game without playing.

In discussing the topic of play with relation to games, four stages of playing should be considered in further defining children's games (Linford and Jeanrenaud). The first is a *preplay* stage: the child has to resolve an approach-avoidance conflict in any new or novel situation. As a teacher you must gradually introduce new play objects or play situations to children. Anything too new or novel may cause them to react with an avoidance mechanism—"I can't do it," "I'm afraid," etc.

After initial exposure the child makes contact with the new play object or initiates activity in the play situation. This stage may be called *specific exploration,* or assimilation, because the child is learning new behaviors. Specific exploration is directed toward identification and determination of the functional characteristics of a stimulus. Specific exploration attempts to answer the questions "What does this object do?" or "What should I do in this situation?" During this stage the child becomes involved with learning the properties of the play object or situation. At this point in time the child manipulates the object or environment to discover the possibilities available. Thus it is important to provide children an opportunity to manipulate balls and other objects in an exploratory or problem-solving manner before playing a game. This coincides with the stages of game playing through which children pass and the teaching approaches to games that teachers may use.

This initial curiosity about manipulative objects or play situations passes into a third stage, which may be called a *conditioned response.* Children tend to repeat those experiences which were positively reinforcing during the exploratory stage. Those experiences which were negatively reinforcing tend to be extinguished. The message is clear. Through careful guidance we must ensure initial positive, satisfying, and successful play experiences for all children. We cannot afford to allow negative reinforcement through fear or failure to cause children to stop playing games.

Positive reinforcement of successful play experiences leads to the fourth stage of *reactive inhibition.* If children continue to play under the same conditions, their behavior loses its stimulating properties as the novelty wears off. To maintain activity or expand it, a person either has to continually look for new possibilities that distort reality or perform at higher levels of ability. This process is sometimes called *diversive exploration,* or accommodation, because activity is directed at variety or toward the generation of new and different sources of stimulation. Diversive exploration seeks to answer the questions "What can I do with this object?" or "What are the different ways of responding in this situation?" Once a child has learned the basics of bouncing a ball, the new challenge is to change speeds, directions, levels, etc. while dribbling the ball like a trick dribbler from the Harlem Globetrotters. A person is also challenged to combine one skill with others as more complex games develop. Within a given game there are continuous attempts to change the rules, strategies, and/or scoring to allow for the increasing ability levels of the players. One has only to look at the professional sports to attest to this—the moving of the goal posts and the punt rule in football, the designated hitter in baseball, and the widening of the free throw lane and the 3-second rule in basketball.

These concepts will be further related to the stages of child development, stages of game playing, and teaching approaches to games as the remainder of this chapter is delineated.

PROCESSES OF PLAY

Children engaged in experiencing the sensory modalities of touch, sight, hearing, taste, and smell can be described as being involved in the process of learning. With respect to play, children learn through the processes of imitation, exploration, prediction, testing, and contesting (Sutton-Smith). They learn about skill development through the process of imitating parents, other adults, peers, and animals. Exploration likewise helps children become familiar with their environment. The process of prediction encourages children to evaluate, analyze, and synthesize the situation in an effort to judge the outcome prior to activity. Games also allow children to engage in the process of testing their skill development and contesting their skill against others. Multisensory awareness through haptic experiences begins through the process of experimenting with concrete situations. As children gain more skill, they delve into abstractions and generalizations. Evidences of this may be witnessed as they engage in the development of language and communication skills, which can be applied to games in the development of rules and strategies.

STAGES OF GAME PLAYING

The stages are classified as follows:

Age (yr)	*Stage*	*Level*	*Process of play*	*Teaching approach*
1 to 5	Egocentric	Self-play Parallel play	Exploration Imitation	Exploration Problem solving
4 to 8	Cooperative	Partner Small group	Imitation Prediction Analysis Synthesis	Problem solving Guided discovery
7 to 12	Competitive	Small group Team	Testing Contesting Analysis Synthesis Evaluation	Problem solving Guided discovery Command

Egocentric stage

At an early age—between 1 and 5 years—children are egocentric in terms of emotional and social development. At the same time they develop initial locomotor, manipulative, and stability movement patterns. Engaged in play, children can best learn these movement patterns while involved in exploratory activities by themselves. Whether learning to manipulate blocks, play in a sandbox, throw a ball, or engage in any other type of activity, children are self-centered. They do not know how to share equipment or take turns. For these reasons, children must have an enriched environment—one in which they may touch, taste, smell, see, and hear a multiplicity of stimuli. In physical education settings the environment should be enriched with different types of balls, hoops, ropes, implements, and similar equipment that children may throw, catch, kick, trap, roll, strike, etc. In addition to exploration, children use imitation and testing in an effort to expand their skills. Problem solving and guided discovery are used as responses vary.

At the same time that children engage in self-play, other children may be engaged in play in the same area. This type of play, termed "parallel play," is defined as children playing in the same area and perhaps even with the same equipment but with different goals or purposes. While one child playing in a sandbox may be building a castle, another may be building a road for a truck. In another situation one child playing with blocks may be building a tower, another may be building his own tower. Because of their egocentricity, if one child needs the other's space, sand, or blocks, there is no reservation in taking them. An argument, loss of temper, or a spat may result. For these same egocentric reasons, children at play in parallel situations need their own equipment and space.

Cooperative stage

After further maturation and learning experiences, children gradually progress to the point at which they can cooperate with others. At first they may begin to play with a partner. At later stages, children may learn to cooperate in small groups of 3 to 6 or even 8.

Play during the cooperative stage is characterized by children working together for a common purpose (Fig. 1-1). The association between partners or players is loose in a rather unstructured manner, with few rules and strategies to bind players together for purposes of competing against another team. Children are still very interested in the development of their own skill.

Cooperative play with a partner may be evidenced by playing catch, kicking and trapping, or striking an object back and forth. Each player is cooperating with the other. The common goal is to help the other in the development of a particular manipulative system. There is no attempt to outplay each other. The simple rule may be just to control the ball.

Small group play during the cooperative stage likewise binds children together for a common purpose. Examples may be playing house—with a mother, father, and sibling; role playing an occupation—doctor, nurse, pa-

Fig. 1-1. Cooperative play.

tient; playing catch; or playing a game of football—hiker, passer, and catcher. In the last two examples, which are most relevant to physical education, competing against another team is not stressed. At best the foe is an imaginary team. The goals are to develop the skills of hiking, passing, throwing, and catching. Children often change positions or roles. Some simple rules or a scoring system may be used as children learn certain basic rules to specific sports. Sometimes younger children play with older ones to learn the rules of games. At other times they become fringe players on teams as they learn about the rules.

During the cooperative stage of partner and small group play, children learn about skill development, rules, and strategies through imitation, prediction, analysis, and synthesis. Cooperation between or among 2 or more children through practice helps build skill development. Social interaction with other children and with teacher-adults through problem solving and guided discovery helps children acquire basic knowledge about the rules and strategies of games. Sharing and learning to take turns are also products of cooperative play.

Competitive stage

With added skill development and the ability to share and cooperate in a group situation, the children move into the competitive play stage (Fig. 1-2). Competitive play during the early stages from 7 to 9 years of age is characterized by 1 to 3 children playing against another small group. Gradually children become more capable of full team play as their skill development

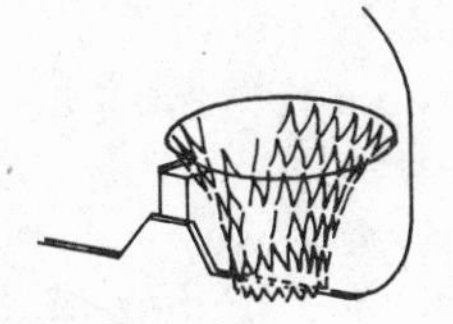

Fig. 1-2. Competitive play.

and understanding of rules and strategies become refined during the upper elementary grades—middle school and beyond.

As children begin team play, a brief look should be taken at their play groups. Normal-sized play groups range from 3 to 6. This allows for maximum participation and involvement in the group. Groups should not be allowed to get too large, since this results in lack of participation or waiting too long for a turn. Games permitting the elimination of players should also be carefully regulated, since often the player who needs the practice and playing experience is eliminated from the game.

At the competitive level, children want to test their skills against those of other children and other teams. They want to learn to play by the rules. They want to do it the "right" way (emulation of the professionals). It is the role of the teacher to provide the proper environment for children to learn to compete and adjust to the various rules and strategies of game playing. With respect to competition, the motivation to compete must be child induced, not adult induced. Children must be allowed to compete with others of similar skill or ability. Children who are forced in some way by adult or peer pressure to compete or who compete with those of a higher ability level are in a compromising position—one in which they may lose and develop a negative self-concept. With respect to learning the rules and strategies of games, children need the chance to become decision makers. Given the chance to analyze, synthesize, and evaluate play situations in a problem-solving or guided discovery situation, the children have many chances to interact with a group and to make decisions concerning the rules and strategies of their games. In a situation in which the teacher makes all the decisions for playing a game in a command manner, the children have little chance to understand the makeup of a game other than to implement the decisions of the teacher. It is my contention that children, given the chance to make decisions about their games, better understand them and make rules that are fair to all participants. Learning the rules and strategies of games in general also helps children adjust to and understand the rules and strategies of the official team games as they are played in later years.

CHILD DEVELOPMENT

The process of play (and stage of game playing in which children are involved) is determined by the stage of child development. A 6-year-old cannot be expected to play the same games as a 12-year-old because of differences in physical, cognitive, emotional, and social developmental factors. It is the purpose of this section of the book to view some important considerations in each category in the light of children's readiness for game playing. Since it is not the purpose of this book to provide a discourse on child development theory, the reader is referred to texts on child psychology for a more complete understanding.

Physical developmental factors

During the elementary school years when children are in the process of developing and refining their manipulative skills, physical developmental factors play an important part in terms of their readiness and performance. Physical fitness factors determine children's ability to perform selected activities. Strength plays an important role in their game-playing skills. Until children are strong enough, equipment may have to be modified to allow for their limited ability to apply force to objects. Nylon rackets may take the place of bats and rackets that are too unwieldly for young children. Small bats, children's golf clubs, and cutoff rackets may enable children with a small amount of strength to successfully engage in eye-hand coordination, striking activities, and games.

Once strength is achieved, especially in boys during the upper elementary years, it enables children to run faster, jump farther, throw harder, and strike with more force. For this reason, children of equal strength should play together. In the primary grades, boys and girls can play together; during the upper elementary grades there may be some instances when it is best to separate the sexes in game activities. Because the endurance of children is often short, activities may have to be interspersed with periods of rest. The development of balance, speed, and agility and the continuation of body flexibility are other fitness factors that need to be considered in the performance of manipulative skills.

Additional obvious physical factors that influence the development of manipulative skills are the weight and size of the children. Other things being equal (especially ability levels), children of equal size and weight should be encouraged to play with each other. Children who are much taller or heavier often gain undue advantage in a game situation. Those who are excessively heavy are also often mismatched in game situations because of their inability to effectively control their body mass. For those children who reach puberty while in the late elementary grades, weight and size may become a problem because of a growth spurt and the resulting inexperience of controlling their new body dimensions.

Perceptual development of the eyes has a marked effect on the performance of children's manipulative skills during the elementary grades. Being able to assess the position, velocity, and acceleration of a moving object determines the efficiency with which they adapt to games. During the early elementary grades, when visual perception is not fully developed, modification of manipulative skills or equipment may allow for successful experiences. A rolling ball, bouncing ball, or slowly floating balloon may help children focus on an object as it comes toward the body. Yarn balls may be used to help them overcome their fear of catching an object. A brightly colored ball may help children learn figure-ground perception. Recent research indicates that accurate judgment of the flight of a moving object cannot be made by children until 11 or 12 years of age. As a result, they should progress from throwing, catching, and striking objects that are in a stationary position to performing with objects in motion. As children gain maturity and experience in manipulative skills, the nervous system adapts in an effort to aid each child to react quickly, assess a situation correctly, and respond efficiently in game-playing situations.

Cognitive concepts

During the elementary school years, children learn cognitive concepts involving knowledge of the facts, comprehension, application, analysis, synthesis, and evaluation (Bloom). Children can learn rules to games by memorizing rules to teacher-designed games or by making up rules to their own games. As they make up rules and strategies to their own games, they must comprehend the game situation, apply rules and strategies to implement their games, and use their decision-making abilities to analyze, synthesize, and evaluate their games according to their ability levels. Also, there will be ample opportunities for children to integrate concepts such as mechanical principles of human movement (science), scoring and court design (mathematics), and speaking, writing, listening, and reading (language arts) in the development of their games.

Emotional development

Among factors regarding emotional development in the affective domain, those which may be most important are self-concept, attention span, stress, use of leisure time, attitudes, and values. During their elementary school years, children develop their self-concept directly and indirectly through many movement experiences in physical education as well as in other life experiences. Those children whose successful experiences outweigh negative experiences tend to develop positive self-images. Those whose negative experiences outweigh the positive experiences tend to develop negative self-images. As a result, activities and games in physical education must be designed to allow for success. Children must also be allowed to play with others of their own ability level so that they have a fair chance for success. Activities in physical education should encourage success so that everyone can feel good about movement. Everyone needs a positive self-concept.

In addition to activities that allow for success, experiences in physical education should be designed to allow for fantasy play as well as risk, daring, and challenge. During fantasy play, children can use their imaginations to play roles of winners, losers, and sports heroes, and the like. They can "try on" life. They can find out who they are and develop empathy for others. Situations that involve a risk or a challenge are necessary to help children find out what they can do. Provided that challenges are within reason, a successful experience with an activity that is daring or involves some element of risk can enhance a child's self-concept.

After working with elementary school children for any period of time, one learns that they all can have a short attention span. This should be kept in mind when planning activities and games. We cannot afford to bore them or try to keep them engaged in play activities in which they are not interested. Indeed, we must allow for changes in activity and make an attempt to let children choose games in which they are interested. Sometimes it is even wise to stop an activity at its peak of interest so that children wish to return to it at a later time.

Factors regarding stress are extremely complex and could demand a whole text in themselves. Basically, some form of competition may be healthy for students at upper elementary levels. Children cannot handle too much stress too early, however. They should be allowed to induce their own competition. Stress created by teachers, parents, and other factors is often harmful. Stress too early is also harmful because children at the egocentric and cooperative levels cannot handle competition well. Only after basic movement patterns and social skills are developed can children test competition drives in a constructive manner.

Projection of the future indicates that individuals will have much leisure time. To cope with this emotionally, they must learn to use their leisure wisely. Helping children learn lifetime sports and play games of their own design—rather than only the team sports, which the average person ceases to play beyond 20 years of age—should help children develop a positive emotional base for valuing sport throughout life. The development of positive attitudes and values toward participation in sport activities stems from a rewarding experience in each of the previously mentioned factors relating to the emotional development of the child.

Social development

The social characteristics of elementary school children vary greatly from the primary grades to the end of the fifth or sixth grade. Prior to entering school, children are egocentric, or self-centered. They do not share well or cooperate with other children easily. In their homes they have been the center of attention and may have coped with only 1 or 2 siblings in the family. Experiences with others in the backyard or neighborhood have been self-oriented with respect to parallel play. Beginning school experiences involving play must bridge the gap between self-orientation and cooperation with and allegiance to peer group members. Taking turns and sharing equipment with a partner helps bridge this gap. Large groups or long relay lines defeat the purpose, however. Playing with another child or a small group of 2 or 3 others for a common goal or purpose helps children learn to communicate with others and gain group acceptance. Being part of a group and contributing physically and/or verbally to it help children learn peer identity, which is so important during the middle elementary school years. Learning to lead the group and also to be a follower are other important aspects of the group experience. Under a traditional setting in which the teacher appoints teams (usually large in size), class captains choose sides, and/or the teacher makes all the decisions for a play experience, children do not get a real chance for group interaction and the resulting social identity. In fact, there are a few children always chosen last who are fringe members and have a negative social experience. As teachers we cannot allow this to happen.

As children improve their social skills through cooperative efforts, they gradually become interested in competitive experiences. Teachers must be careful to guide children so that socially some do not overly dominate others. If children can be allowed to compete with others of their own ability level in self-designed games, each child has a good chance of social acceptance. When large or unequal teams compete under stressful conditions created by adults and with undue pressure from adults, some children have a negative social experience. For a child, being told that he is no good or is not wanted on the team or being laughed at and ridiculed is not a positive social experience. These situations should not be allowed to occur. Children must be taught sportsmanship and to compliment others for honest, hard effort. Children must be allowed to cooperate and compete with others of equal ability so that everyone has a chance for success.

An outgrowth of these cooperative and competitive social experiences is the development of an ethical and moral code. Within a given play situation, matters such as crime, deception, rules, judges, codes of law, jurisprudence, and taken-for-granted understandings arise. There is an interplay between freedom and responsibility. Rather than an attitude of win at all costs, it would be much wiser to help children develop respect for rules and a desire to play within them. By constructing play environments through problem solving, children may construct, interpret, negotiate, argue over, debate about, and on occasion suspend or abandon rules. Children can thus learn that rules bring order to a situation and that rules specify rights, obligations, duties, and privileges. Ultimately children should learn that respect for authority, seriousness of intent, rules, competition, cooperation, and common understandings are basic to any sustained social endeavor (friendship, marriage, vocation, etc.).

CONCEPTUAL APPROACH TO GAMES

Traditional curricular approaches to games are usually divided into units that focus on a particular sport. In these units a teacher chooses to spend a specified amount of time or number of class periods during which children learn skills that may be applied in a game. In this type of content approach the game, the competition, or the concentration on winning often becomes the focus of attention. When this happens, the teacher and children often lose sight of the fact that in the elementary school the game is a means to an end. The process of concentrating on skill development is the real purpose or goal of physical education. To put this into proper perspective, there has been a recent emphasis on curriculum development toward a conceptual approach to physical education and game playing (Gallahue et al.; Seidel et al.).

Human movement may be divided into three broad categories or concepts: stability, locomotion, and manipulation.

Concepts of human movement

Stability	*Locomotion*	*Manipulation*
Bending	Walking	Throwing
Stretching	Running	Catching
Twisting	Jumping	Carrying
Rotating	Hopping	Kicking
Swinging	Skipping	Trapping
Standing	Galloping	Striking
Inverted support	Leaping	Volleying
Rolling	Climbing	Bouncing
Landing	Sliding	Rolling
Stopping		
Dodging		

As children learn fundamental movement patterns at initial levels, each of these concepts may be taught in isolation through the teaching methods of exploration, problem solving, guided discovery, and command, which are discussed later in the chapter. Gradually, these concepts may be combined, and combined skills may be implemented in game playing. Indeed, every game that is played is a combination or conceptual skills. For example, in basketball a player bends, stretches, twists, etc. (stability) as he runs, jumps, hops, etc. (locomotion) or dribbles, passes, shoots, etc. (manipulation) the ball.

Within the context of the conceptual curriculum the focus of children's games becomes the process of learning skills and not the game itself. Thus, if the development of throwing and catching is the primary focus, the teacher and/or children may choose to play any game in which these skills are used (football, softball, basketball). They may even choose to invent a new game that stresses one or more concepts in a process approach.

The development of game-playing skills obviously stresses the process of learning to manipulate objects. Therefore the remainder of this section will concern the development of manipulative concepts (shown below). As each of the chapters on manipulative concepts is delineated, concepts of stability and locomotion are naturally combined and integrated at appropriate times.

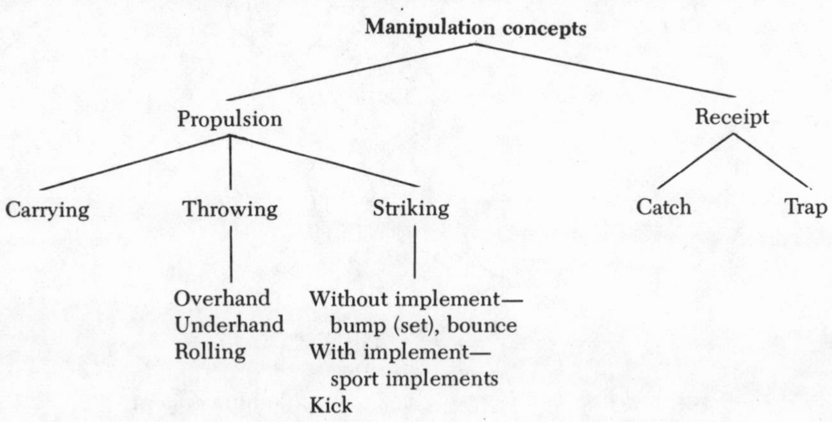

Manipulative concepts may be divided into two subcategories: one in which the body gives force to an object and one in which the body receives force from an object. When a person gives force to an object, it is called propulsion. Basic propulsive concepts are carrying, throwing, and striking. Throwing and striking can each be further broken down into subconcepts. When a person receives force from an object, it is called receipt. Basic receipt concepts are catching and trapping. (See diagram on p. 13.)

Propulsion concepts

Carrying (Fig. 1-3)

Carrying is a unique manipulative concept in which an object stays in continuous contact with the human body. A person carrying an object uses skills of stopping, starting, and agility to elude an opponent, to advance the object on the playing surface, and/or to cross a goal.

Throwing

Throwing is a concept in which force is imparted to an object. In the process of throwing, the hand holds the object continuously while the body gradually builds up momentum. The object is finally propelled into space on release. The act of throwing may be an overhand, underhand (toss), or sidearm movement. The object may be thrown in various directions and with various speeds for distance or accuracy.

Fig. 1-3. Carrying is a manipulation concept.

Rolling

Rolling is a specialized form of throwing in which the object is placed on the floor or ground as it is released.

Striking

As in throwing, striking is a concept in which force is imparted to an object. The differences between the two concepts lie in the buildup of momentum and the amount of time in contact with the object. Unlike throwing, the buildup of momentum in the body is made prior to and without contact with the object. After a maximum buildup of momentum, the body makes only momentary contact with the object in a ballistic motion. The striking movement may be made with an implement (tennis, golf, baseball, etc.) (Fig. 1-4) or without one (handball, kick, etc.). It may be made with the head (heading), arms (volley, bump [set]), knee, or feet (kick).

Bouncing, or dribbling

Bouncing, or dribbling, is a form of striking in which an object is repeatedly pushed down at the ground.

Bump, or set

The bump, or set, is a specialized form of striking in which the ball is hit into the air in a vertical direction without touching the ground.

Fig. 1-4. Striking with an implement gives force to objects.

Implement

The use of an implement such as a bat, racket, or club in various types of sports to impart force to an object is a striking action. Underhand, sidearm, overhand, forehand, and backhand motions are made as objects are struck in vertical and/or horizontal projectiles with much or little force.

Kicking

Kicking is a specialized form of striking in which the foot imparts momentum to an object. In the process of kicking, the foot and leg build up momentum before striking the object. Contact with the object is only momentary. Kicking may be done with either leg. Objects may be kicked in various directions and pathways with different amounts of force, and for distance or accuracy. (See Fig. 1-5).

Receipt concepts

Catching

Catching is a concept in which the force of an object is received by the body. In the process of catching, usually the hands receive the impact of the object as the wrists, elbows, and shoulders help absorb the blow by bending. When catching an object at a high level, the thumbs are close together with the fingers pointing up; when catching an object at a low level, the little fingers are close together with the fingers pointing down.

Fig. 1-5. Kicking is a form of striking.

Trapping

Trapping is a concept similar to catching, in which the force of an object is absorbed by the body. Trapping may be accomplished with the abdomen, leg, and/or foot.

TYPES OF GAMES

Games that people play may be classified by type—closed and open. A *closed game* may be one in which the situation is predictable or predetermined. A game or contest in bowling (Fig. 1-6) or archery is predetermined by distance from the target and scoring. The target is stationary and the performer needs to learn to aim correctly to hit it. Many children's games at an early stage of specific exploration are characterized by their closed nature. A child's first attempt at any new manipulative skill will be most successful in a situation in which the child and/or the target is stationary and the outcome is predictable.

Whereas some games maintain a closed framework even at high levels of competition, many (especially team games) can be classified as open. An *open game* is one in which the situation is unpredictable or not predetermined. A basketball player dribbling downcourt has to make an on-the-spot decision to drive in for a lay-up, pass to a teammate, stop and shoot from the outside, or set up an offensive play. In this example or those involving tennis, soccer, football, and other sports, the situation is continually changing. After a period of specific exploration and learning to control the object itself, children become ready for diversive exploration. Given the ability to bounce, shoot, and/or pass the ball, the child is ready to make game decisions regarding rules and strategies. During the upper elementary school years, children should be

Fig. 1-6. Bowling is a closed game.

exposed to many types of open game situations in which they can test their manipulative skills in a variety of unpredictable circumstances.

TEACHING APPROACHES TO GAMES

After defining play and considering the stages of game playing, the various aspects of child development, a conceptual approach to movement, and types of games, we must turn to the act of teaching itself. How do teachers present manipulative movement patterns and games to children? According to one appraisal (Dochtery and Peake), teachers can use a creative or traditional approach to teaching games to children. According to another (Riley), the games we teach children reflect the amount of teacher-child interaction. There are games that are totally teacher determined and directed, games in which the teacher and children interact to make up and modify the rules, and also games in which the children are given the opportunity to make up their own rules without teacher intervention. A review of the literature shows that various other authors (Mosston; Gilliom) have identified over seven teaching methods which a physical education teacher may use.

Because this book is primarily about games, it is the purpose of this section to briefly review selected teaching methods and indicate how they can be used to enhance the development of game-playing skills in children. The teaching methods that will be considered are exploration, problem-solving, guided discovery, and command. Each of the methods presented is not good or bad in itself but must be considered in relation to the definition of play, stage of child development, stage of game playing, and particular manipulative concept or game being taught. Only then can wise decisions be made regarding the methods that should be used to teach games to children.

Exploration

As a teaching method, exploration is most difficult to define because of wide misinterpretation of the use of freedom. Within the exploratory teaching method the teacher poses questions and challenges that allow the children to move freely with reference to the qualities, or elements, of movement. (See Fig. 1-7.) Initially, children explore the qualities of movement with reference to their own bodies. They move through personal and general space in terms of exploring space, force, time, and flow (Laban notation). Focus is directed toward body movements and the relationships the body creates with objects and other people as the children learn how and where the body moves. This does not mean, however, that children are free to do whatever they wish. They are allowed to move within the stipulation of the situation posed by the teacher. If the students are asked to explore hopping movements with reference to directional and pathway changes, and one child chooses to run or jump, he is outside the limits of the problem. His efforts need to be redirected.

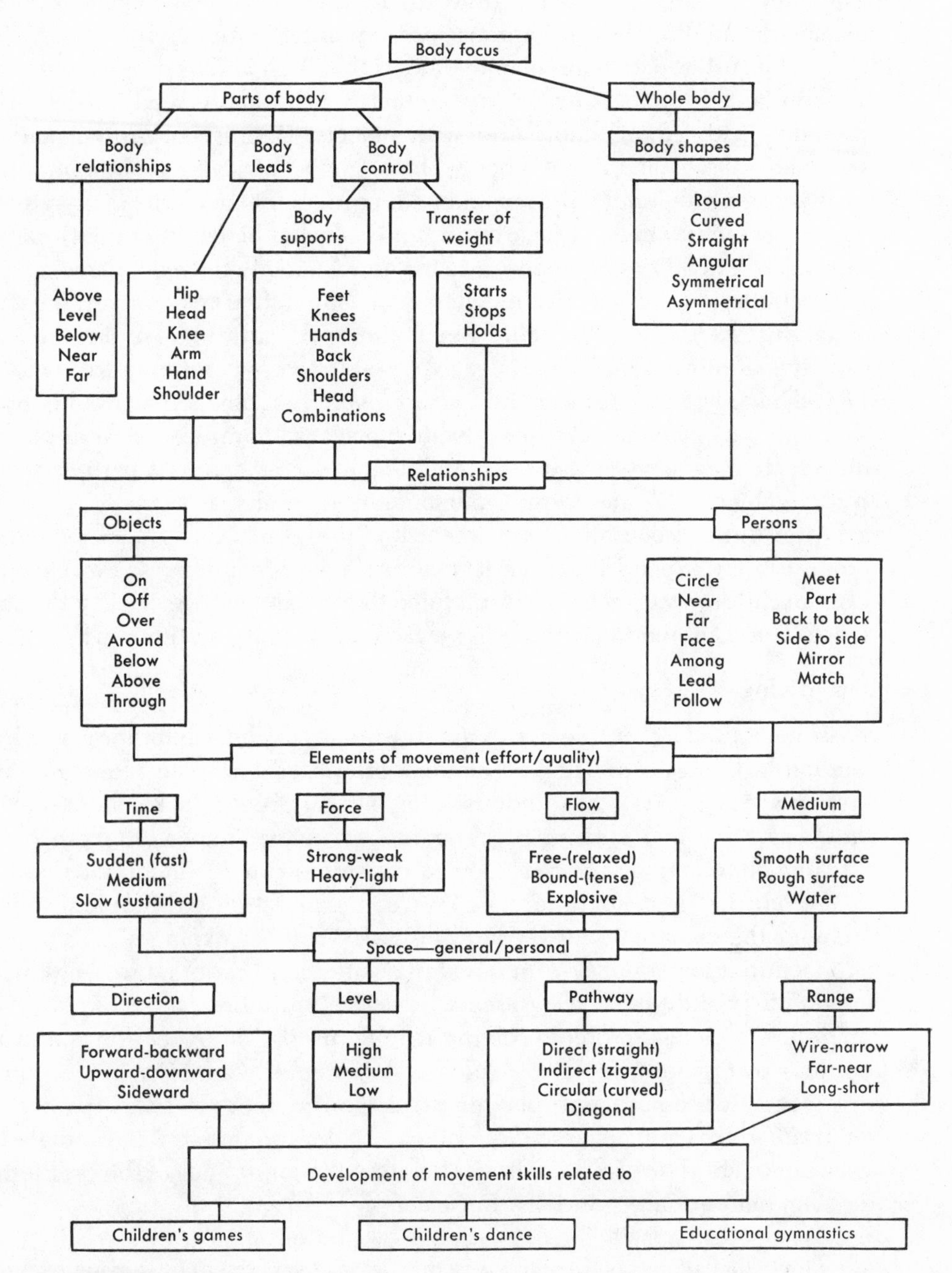

Fig. 1-7. Development of basic movement patterns through exploration, discovery, and problem solving.

The children also are asked to move by themselves unless requested by the teacher or another child to interact with a partner or small group.

As the children explore the movements that their bodies can make through stability and locomotor experiences, they become more ready to begin exploration with other people and with objects. Because of growth and developmental characteristics and a child's egocentric development, initial experiences with other children and with equipment should be exploratory in nature. The child needs to learn the limits of what he can do in each new or novel play situation. He needs to learn how his body moves with relation to other children and objects as he enters into cooperative and competitive game situations. As a result, the child needs the opportunity to explore the same qualities of movement he initially explored to learn about his own body. He may change the direction, pathway, and level of an object (ball) as he moves through space. He may change the rate (speed) and application of force to an object. He may move side by side and near or far away from a partner as they pass an object back and forth in personal or general space.

After initial isolation of movement qualities, combinations of movement qualities may expand into a variety of exploratory challenges. For example, can the children vary the speed and force they use to bounce a ball at the same time? The combinations are endless. How many can you think of?

Problem solving

The method of problem solving is similar to the exploratory teaching method in that questions and situations are posed to the children in which there may be a variety of solutions. They remain free to make choices about their cognitive and movement behavior. As in exploration, the process of thinking, interacting, and variation is considered more important than the final product. The major difference between exploration and problem solving includes the complexity or level of the task. Whereas exploration refers to a child's initial experiences with novel play situations, problem solving relates more to the conditioned response and reactive inhibition stages of play. With reference to games, problem solving may be used to allow children to make up their own games, including rules and strategies. Combinations of movement qualities, equipment, playing areas, and partner relationships may be determined by the teacher and/or children. After the problem is stipulated, it is up to the child (or children) to work within the guidelines of the problem to develop one or more solutions. For example:

> Given a ball and a hoop, make up a game by yourself or with a partner in which the ball passes through the hoop. You may vary the force, speed, level, and direction of the ball as you throw, kick, or strike it.

The problem is stated; it is up to the children, depending on their stage of game playing, to make decisions about rules, strategies, scoring, and other game variables. The game may be simple or cooperative in nature, or it may be complex and competitive. The list of problem statements is unlimited when various manipulative patterns are combined with movement qualities and game strategies.

Guided discovery

One of the common criticisms, misconceptions, or misunderstandings about creative teaching methods and approaches to learning skills and playing games is that in open-ended problems the children do not get enough guidance concerning effective ways to perform. After all, how is a child expected to learn to throw, catch, kick, or guard an opponent if all he does is experiment with a variety of solutions to the problems? Once the child has been introduced to a play situation and has been allowed to explore a variety of alternatives to a given movement experience, he needs to learn mechanically efficient ways to execute skills and strategically effective ways to play games. Guided discovery is the teaching method that allows and encourages this learning.

The process of guided discovery is similar to exploration and problem solving during initial stages in that the teacher may use questions and challenges as the children experiment with various possibilities in any given movement situation. However, after the initial period of experimentation in a rather open-ended situation, the teacher cues in on the children's actions and poses further questions and challenges in an attempt to get them to discover a concept related to movement or strategies of play. Although the beginning questions and challenges may be general in nature, the teacher leads the children through a process of discovering something specific. Examples within the areas of manipulation and game playing are learning about the base of support; using mechanically efficient methods of performing the throw, catch, kick, strike, etc.; or moving to an open space to receive the ball. However, instead of being told how to perform, as in the command style of teaching, the children are given the opportunity to discover the answers for themselves.

In this manner it is believed that children learn best those things with which they have to deal cognitively through comprehension, application, analysis, synthesis, and evaluation. When the teacher gives the children a specific method of performance, the children have no reason to learn the how's and why's of performance at their conscious level. All they have to do is accept whatever the teacher tells them.

Command

The command, or traditional, method is perhaps most easy to identify with because it has been used predominantly over the years. The teacher has a plan of action and a rather structured or orderly method of execution. The teacher gives specific instructions through lecture or demonstration. Then the children go through a period of practice or game playing in predetermined formations. This particular teaching method has advantages in time efficiency and directness when a specific skill or game is to be learned. Its major criticisms lie in the question of being teacher or child centered. If we believe in the value of giving children the opportunity to use their cognitive powers and become involved in the decision-making process, we may consider using the three previous teaching methods as much as possible, and reserving the command method for use only when time, efficiency, and directness dictate.

ETHOLOGY OF PLAY

Browne published some significant information regarding the science of ethology—the study of animal behavior—in relation to human behavior in sport. It seems appropriate at this time to review that information in relation to the play experiences of children. Recognizing that all animals (including humans) play, we may begin to apply some principles in an attempt to analyze common factors with regard to play behavior. The first principle is *territory*. All play behavior, including games, holds territory in high esteem. The exploration of personal and general space in movement exploration is the essence of discovering one's territory. Traditional children's games are replete with examples of territorial definition: king on the mountain, hide and seek, prisoner's base, and capture the flag. Under careful scrutiny one can divide these games by category according to the formation used. Some games have circular formations, and others have line or scatter formations. Examples of games defined by formation follow.

Formation of games

Circle	*Line*	*Scatter*
Drop the handkerchief	Midnight	The hunt
Duck, duck, goose	Hill dill	Squirrel in the tree
Run home	Crows and cranes	Loose caboose
Three deep	Red rover	Tag games
Dodge ball	Dodge ball	Norwegian ball
	Steal the bacon	

The boundaries of a game or the actual playing area can be used to further define territory. Some games are played in an area that is mutually occupied by members of each team. They are called field games. Examples are football, basketball, and racquetball. In other games, called net games, the teams are separated and remain on opposite sides of the play area throughout the game. Any time a player crosses to the opposing side of the playing area, this constitutes a foul or rule violation. Examples of net games are volleyball, badminton, and tennis.

Fig. 1-8. King of the mountain is a territorial game.

Implicit in the principle of territory is the concept that animals fight the hardest to defend their territory as the enemy approaches the heart of their homeland. The aggressor tends to lose his aggression the farther he is from his own territory. This forms the basis of the "goal line stand" in football and favoring the team playing on its home ground. (See Fig. 1-8.)

The concepts of game formations and playing areas are further considered in the section on rules and strategies of game playing later in this chapter. It is proposed that among other factors, children should be free to choose a particular formation or playing area as they design their own games.

To continue with the principles of ethology, we must consider *pecking order,* the second principle, to be an aspect of play and sport. As evidenced by the dominant buck in a herd of deer or the hierarchy of the military, we can clearly see that both animals and man have ranking systems concerning the order of importance. Other examples drawn from various vocations and sporting activities follow.

Hierarchical classifications

University teacher	*Factory*	*Professional sports*	*Olympics*	*Little League*
Dean	Boss	World champion	Olympic champion	National champion
Chairman of department	Division manager	Conference champion	World class	Regional champion
Professor	Manager	Playoffs	Preolympic	State champion
Associate professor	Foreman	Division champion	AAU-NCAA	City champion
Assistant professor	Skilled worker	Major League	College	League competition
Instructor	Laborer	Minor League	High school	T ball

Although recognizing that the principle of pecking order permeates human lives, we must put into perspective the extent to which it affects the lives of children. Since children are not miniature adults, they cannot handle the same stresses and pressures that adults do. The stresses imposed by grades and competition are sometimes too much for children, especially if the stresses are adult imposed. This comes to light in many of the traditional games taught to children. To begin with, two recognized leaders choose their teams. The children of lesser skill, the smallest, and/or the youngest get chosen last, putting them at the bottom of the pecking order. They are told to play a position where they will seldom handle the ball. If a ball comes their way, a child with greater skill rushes to the ball and plays it. If the child with lesser skill makes a mistake, he is ridiculed by the other team as well as his own teammates. In games that require serving or striking the ball, this same child is the last in line to get a turn. With short class periods there is a question whether he will get a turn at all. With the substitute, or designated hitter, rule, it is possible to have a person with greater skill take his turn—all for the purpose of winning the game. But what are we doing to the child's self-concept?

Other games include elimination of players who are unskilled. It is precisely these players who need to stay in the game to develop their skills. This survival of the fittest attitude again destroys the self-concept of the average and below-average players.

In an attempt to follow the trends of elementary school education regarding open education, personalized learning, nongraded classrooms, individually guided education, and multi-age, multigraded classes, we should carefully guide the games children play with respect to pecking order. That is not to say we should deny or avoid the fact that pecking order exists. But we should allow children to design games in which they can participate at their

Fig. 1-9. Manipulative equipment is a symbolic weapon in game play.

skill level and be successful. As their skill level increases, their level of competition also increases. As they move toward adolescence and high school, they will gradually become more ready for the pressures of pecking order that they will face as adults at a time when they can better cope with it.

Weaponry is the third principle of ethology that clearly affects play for humans and primates. Many sporting events today consist of the use of implements important in war during past history. The javelin (spear), bow and arrow, discus, fencing foils, and rifles are obvious examples. Other sports clearly employ weapon substitutes. The club used in golf and hockey, the bat in baseball, and the racket in tennis and badminton can all be considered weapons (Fig. 1-9). Even the ball—or any other object, for that matter—may be considered a weapon. In baseball the pitcher uses the ball to throw through the opposition's territory. If successful, he can put out his adversary and keep his team secure. On the other hand, the batter who can use his weapon to propel the ball into the opponent's territory or over the fence can conquer the opposition by circling his territory and rendering him helpless.

The ball is equally important as a weapon in other sports such as football. The ball is the key to penetration of the opponent's territory. The ball is the key to combat as it is passed, carried, kicked, or intercepted. Can you think of other examples in which balls are used as weapons in sports?

As an interesting sidelight to the principle of weaponry, the size and type of implements that children use in the games they play must also be considered. It would be absurd to think that humans in past history taught their children to use adult-sized weapons until they were ready for them. Instead, children played with smaller-sized or modified versions until they could handle the real weapons. It is just as absurd to see our young children of today using professional model gloves, bats, rackets, and similar equipment. What they really need is modified equipment to use during the developmental skill process. Then, as they become older and stronger, they can switch to the official equipment. This topic is further considered in the next section on equipment for all children.

Because of the process of evolution, humans today give expression to these ethological principles through the social institutions of play and pageantry. In the animal kingdom, territorial battles, play, and courting are carried out by strict rules to prevent intraspecies killing. In sporting contests, too, strict rules are enforced by officials, and it is by these rules that children must be taught to live. Therefore, in planning the play experiences of children, it would be wise to consider the principles of territory, pecking order, and weaponry. The closer that activities in physical education come to defining these principles, the more successful we may be in preparing youth for the real world they will enter as adults.

EQUIPMENT FOR ALL CHILDREN

In many public schools, large classes and/or lack of facilities and equipment often causes problems in effectively teaching movement experiences to children in the elementary school, especially in the primary grades. Large classes prevent children from having adequate time to explore and manipulate various pieces of equipment because they must wait their turn. In classes in which only one or two pieces of equipment can be found, children get caught in the waiting process also. As a result, they are robbed of quantitative and qualitative movement experiences that would allow for the development of manipulative patterns through game activities. In addition, discipline and control problems often result when children have to wait in lines.

In an attempt to provide a solution to such problems, teachers and parents should be encouraged to develop homemade physical education equipment. The nature of homemade equipment stresses the amount of adaptation for use by all children. Changes in the size, weight, shape, etc. of specific pieces of equipment make them more usable by children—young and old, large and small. For example, yarn balls may be employed with children who have eye-hand coordination problems and are afraid to catch a regular ball for fear of getting hurt. Balloons or beach balls may be used when it is important to increase the size of the ball or to slow its flight. Nylon rackets may be used when a bat or tennis racket is too large, heavy, and unmanageable for a young child.

The use of free and inexpensive materials allows each child to explore various movement patterns as an individual or in a small group. Innovative equipment is especially adaptable to movement education situations during the primary grades. Children should be encouraged to explore the various movement qualities of space, force, time, and flow as they experience manipulative activities.

Innovative equipment may also be adapted for use in lead-up games to team sports and other movement experiences. It is not, however, the intent of this book to "play down" the importance of regular equipment for physical education. A combination of innovative and manufactured equipment is important to a quality physical education program from kindergarten through grade 12.

For further information on equipment for all children, see Werner and Simmons.

RULES AND STRATEGIES OF GAME PLAYING

Given a ball, a bat, a Frisbee, or any other piece of play equipment, adults are seldom at a loss when they desire to play. For the most part, unless adults become involved in league play, they play in small groups with friends. They play catch with a friend. They play with 3 (cutthroat), 2 against 2, 3 against 3, or in one small group (work-up). Adults make up rules regarding boundaries, scoring, time, strategies, penalties, and other game factors to fit their special conditions. If a rule does not work out, they are sensible enough to change it during the game. If a game appears to mismatch opponents or if the rules are inequitable to one of the teams, adjustments are made before a new game is started.

Yet seldom do adults give children credit for the ability to make the same decisions. A teacher chooses a game such as kickball or dodge ball with predetermined rules for the children to play. The children are divided into large groups (5 or more), usually by squads or by choosing sides—a concept that is itself inhumane because invariably the least capable performers get chosen last, thereby defeating their self-concept. The rules are explained by the teacher, using a command style of teaching. As a result, the children are banned from the decision-making process with regard to members of the team, the game itself, rules of the game, level of competition, scoring, etc. Following the explanation of the rules, the game is played. Whether the children like the game, whether it is successful, and whether their ability levels are challenged are usually ignored because it is the *product*, or game, that is considered important.

It is the thesis of this book that the process is the most important aspect of game playing. By taking into account the stages of child development, the stages of game playing, a concept approach to games, and the various teaching

FACTORS COMMON TO GAMES

Formation
Circle
Line
Scatter

Playing area
Field
Net

Equipment
Balls, different kinds
Hoop
Rope
Racket
Bat
Tire
Scoop
Target

Time
Whole game
- Quarter
- Half
- Period
- Inning
- Set

Play segment
- 3 seconds
- 10 seconds
- 24 seconds

Score
Object in goal or target
Object struck into field
Object over or under net

Points scored
Start with number and subtract
1, 2, 3, 4, 5, 6 for each score

Rules, fouls, and penalties

Attempts
- 1 try
- 2 tries
- 3 tries
- 4 tries

Position of object
- On ground
- In air
  - Above knee
  - Below shoulder
  - Above shoulder
- In or out of play
  - Object inside or outside boundary
  - Object hits floor 1 or 2 times

Fouls
- Holding
- Tripping
- Roughness
- Blocking
- Screening
- Moving too soon
- Carrying ball
- Starting before ball in play
- Cannot be into, over, or under net
- Cannot be ahead of ball as player advances downfield

Penalties
- Free throw
- Free kick
- Side out
- Out of game

methods previously outlined, teachers can guide or set the stage for children to develop their own games according to their ability levels and interests. By providing a framework within which to work, children can be allowed to make their own game decisions. After choosing a movement concept and the qualities of movement previously outlined, teachers should allow the children choices regarding the factors common to games. For example, after the teacher chooses striking at a level above the hips in a vertical direction, children should be allowed to choose small groups of their own and make up their own game by varying the factors common to games. (See p. 28.) One group might choose a circular formation, and others might choose a scatter formation. They might choose a net or field orientation. Equipment might be chosen or designated by the teacher. The groups can choose rules for time, scoring, fouls, penalties, and other game factors in a similar manner. The end result is a process in which children invent their own games. Some games will work. Others will not. The latter will either be scrapped or modified until they do work. The important ingredients are the children's efforts to mold movement concepts into games of their own design and the cognitive and emotional-social development encouraged in the process of game design. It is hoped that this approach will effectively contribute to the development of future adults who are capable of doing new things, are creative and inventive, and are discoverers.

• • •

Chapters 2 to 4 are devoted to the development of game concepts for children with respect to their stages of development. The concepts of throwing and catching, kicking and trapping, and striking with and without implements will be discussed individually relative to the cooperative and competitive levels of game playing and appropriate teaching methods to accomplish these objectives. The last chapter concerns other game concepts and combinations of movement concepts that can be developed with children.

The format of each chapter is initiated by a discussion of the developmental principles and stages that children follow while learning each of the manipulative concepts. Next, exploratory challenges and problem-solving and guided discovery problems are given in an attempt to help children through the initial processes of play involving specific exploration, self-play, parallel play, and small-group cooperative play. After children have gained some skill in each of the manipulative concepts, cooperative and competitive game situations with some sample games are developed to guide children through the stages of diversive exploration and cooperative and competitive play in which they can use cognitive and social strategies in game implementation. In all the game examples, readers are encouraged to identify each of the factors common to games. Which games are open or closed? Which games are cooperative or competitive? Which are net or field oriented? How many players are on each team? How are points scored? How much is each score worth? What are the rules of the game? What are the penalties for infractions? Last comes the real challenge. After using the guidelines developed herein, teachers should develop their own games for children, or better yet, *guide the children and allow them to develop their own games* as a result of progressing from original games toward conventional-type games.

CHAPTER TWO

Throwing and catching

Just like the age-old question of which came first, the chicken or the egg, it may be conjecture whether the ability to throw or catch develops first. Actually, they develop somewhat simultaneously. The fundamental movement patterns of throwing and catching involve the propulsion of an object away from the body and the reception of an object by the body. From the time children are able to throw and catch, one often hears them say "Let's play a game of catch" or, more simply, "Let's play catch." For this play transaction to occur, they must be involved in the skills of throwing and catching. It is difficult to separate the two skills because when one occurs, usually the other follows. As a result, both skills will be developed in this chapter as a way to enhance games that involve throwing and catching.

PRINCIPLES OF HUMAN DEVELOPMENT

From the time a small infant lies in his crib or is propped up in a chair and makes his initial attempts to contact an object within his reach, the skills of prehension begin to develop from reflex actions. Principles of human development affect children's attempts to reach for, grasp, and release objects. Reaching for and grasping objects may be considered initial attempts at catching. Releasing objects may be considered throwing. An infant playing with a rattle may reach for it and grasp it gleefully. Yet after a short period of time, that same infant may be seen crying while shaking the same rattle. Because of the principle of flexion-extension, the infant's flexor muscles are more fully developed than are the extensor muscles, and, as a result, he cannot let go of the rattle. The same flexor-extensor principle may be applied throughout early childhood because most youngsters are unreliable at aiming an object at a target when throwing.

In addition to the flexor-extensor principle, other principles of human development affect learning the associated skills of throwing and catching. Children's large muscles develop before they gain control over their smaller muscles. Their muscles also develop from the center of the body to the periphery (proximodistal development). Both concepts affect children's abilities to throw and catch an object. As children gain experience and maturity, their throws are controlled more by their fine motor (refined) release at the periphery of the body (long lever arm). Their catches, too, progress from being handled by the trunk and large muscles, with a scooping action of the arms or a trap by the arms against the trunk, to gaining manual control over the object.

Another principle that affects throwing and catching is unilateral-contralateral development. A child's initial attempts at throwing involve unilateral development. A right-handed child initially steps forward with the right foot (the foot on the same side of the body). Gradually he changes over to the more mature pattern of stepping forward with the opposite foot. A child's initial attempts at catching involve either no foot movement or a step backward. Gradually he steps forward to meet the oncoming object.

Principles of the development of visual perception likewise affect a child's ability to manipulate an object. Initial farsightedness hinders a child's ability to focus on an object as he prepares to catch it. The eye-hand coordination required to catch a moving object develops gradually during the elementary school years, until at 11 or 12 years of age a child is finally able to reliably catch a moving object while he himself is on the move. Visual figure-ground perception also plays an important role in the development of manipulative skills. In general, objects such as balls that are used for purposes of throwing and catching should provide a good contrast with the background. For example, a white object against a green background or a dark object against a light background provides a good contrast so that the primary stimulus stands out from the background.

THROWING

As separate skills, throwing and catching mature progressively within the range of these principles of human and perceptual development until proficiency is achieved. Throwing seems to develop at a somewhat faster rate,

Fig. 2-1. Different styles of throwing.

since studies show that 80% of 5-year-old children are able to throw in a mature fashion, whereas only 56% of 5-year-olds can catch in a mature fashion.

By definition, throwing is an act that involves applying force to an object. In the process of throwing, the hand holds the object continuously while the body gradually builds up momentum. The object is finally propelled into space on release.

There are many varieties of throwing: overhand, underhand (toss), or rolling motion (Fig. 2-1). But regardless of the form of the throw, children seem to pass through three stages on their way to a mature throwing pattern. The first, termed the *initial* stage, is characterized by a throw from the elbow with little or no trunk and foot action. No shift in weight takes place during the throwing process. It is almost a push of the object away from the body. The second, or *elementary,* stage involves the whole arm and includes a windup, or preparatory, and follow-through phases. Some trunk rotation occurs, but it is limited by stepping forward with the leg on the same side of the body as the throwing arm. The third, or *mature,* stage involves a summation of forces from the whole body. The leg on the opposite side of the throwing arm is extended, offering a wide base of support, as well as providing some initial forward momentum. The momentum is transferred to the trunk, which, as it rotates, provides additional force. All this force is then transferred from the body to the arm as the elbow leads the throwing motion, followed by a force application by the wrist and fingers as the ball leaves the hand.

As children learn to throw by using the various forms, their experiences should be varied in an attempt to develop a pattern that is adaptable in many game situations. They should manipulate large, medium, and small balls of different sizes, shapes, and textures. Yarn balls, tennis balls, playground balls, footballs, and bowling balls should be used in an appropriate manner to help children learn to throw for form, accuracy, and distance. They should be encouraged to throw from different levels and in different directions. Children should first learn to throw an object while standing still before learning to throw while moving. In various circumstances they should learn to throw equally well with either or both hands. They should also vary the trajectory of the object, the amount of force applied, and speed with which the object is thrown prior to applying their skill in a game situation.

At times, throwing is accomplished by using an implement to apply force to objects (jai alai, lacrosse). Children can use plastic scoops and similar modified equipment to learn how to use implements to apply force to objects. Later they can apply their skill in game situations.

Rolling a ball or another object is a form of throwing that is used during early childhood and is continued in some kinds of games throughout life (bowling). Sliding a ball or an object, too, is a form of throwing that is used in some types of games (shuffleboard). Each skill should be developed and explored in much the same manner as throwing so that they can be refined and implemented in games later in childhood and throughout life.

CATCHING

Like throwing, catching also is a multifaceted skill. The general category of catching includes the absorption of the force of an object that is rolling, bouncing, or airborne. The ability to catch develops during early childhood in stages that follow the principles of human development and of perceptual development. The first stage, sometimes called a "basket catch," involves the use of the whole arm and the trunk. The ball is actually trapped by the arms against the trunk. The arms are tense, and there is little use of the hands during the catch. The catch is poorly timed, and a withdrawal or avoidance reaction of the head may occur because the child may be unable or afraid to follow the path of the ball with the eyes. During the second stage the child makes some attempt to catch the object with the hands, although timing may remain poor and the object still may be trapped against the body. During the third stage a mature catching pattern is achieved. The hands are used to catch the object away from the body, although the arms may be drawn in toward the body to absorb force from the object. If the object is above the chest, the fingers are pointed up, with the thumbs held close together in preparation for catching the object. If the object is below the waist, the fingers are pointed down, with the little fingers held close together. (See Fig. 2-2.) Once the mature stage of catching is achieved, there is no longer an avoidance reaction because the eyes can now follow an object during its complete flight phase.

As children learn to catch, their experiences should be varied in an attempt to develop a pattern that is adaptable in many game situations. They should experience catching objects of different sizes, weights, shapes, colors, and textures. Children should catch balls that have traveled different distances,

Fig. 2-2. Catching at different levels.

have been thrown with varying amounts of force, and are traveling at different speeds. They should first learn to catch an object while in a stationary position and progress to catching an object while on the move. They should also catch balls at different levels and from different trajectories prior to applying their skill in a game situation.

In addition, children should be given opportunities to catch objects through the use of implements. Baseball gloves, lacrosse cradles, plastic scoops, tin cans, etc. can all be used to emphasize the concept of efficient absorption of force. When using implements to catch objects, children should go through the same sequences as previously outlined for catching without implements.

THROWING AND CATCHING ACTIVITIES THROUGH EXPLORATION AND PROBLEM SOLVING

Individual

1. Find a ball and get it into your own space. With only a little force throw the ball up just a short distance and catch it.
2. Can you throw it up with both hands and catch it with both? Can you throw it up with the right hand and catch it with the right? Left to left? Right to left? Left to right?
3. Can you throw it up at a low level and catch it at a low level? Can you throw it up at a high level and catch it at a high level? Low level to high level? High level to low level?
4. Increase the amount of force you apply to the ball, making it go higher and

higher. How high can you throw it under control and catch it without moving from your own space?

5. How many different ways can you throw the ball up in the air? How many different ways can you catch the ball?
6. Can you throw the ball up in the air, turn around, and catch it before it bounces on the floor? Can you turn around twice before catching it?
7. Can you throw the ball up and clap your hands before you catch it? How many times can you clap before you catch it?
8. Can you jump into the air and throw the ball? While you are in the air, can you throw the ball vertically, horizontally, at a target, with different amounts of force, etc.? Can you jump into the air and catch the ball?
9. Repeat the above activities by using all different types of objects to throw and catch. Vary their size, weight, shape, color, texture, etc. Play catch with footballs, nerfballs, yarn balls, Frisbees, basketballs, etc.
10. Can you throw the ball up in the air and take a specific number of steps (one, two, three, four, etc.) before you catch it?
11. Can you throw the ball up in the air and let it bounce a specific number of bounces (one, two, three, four, etc.) before you catch it?
12. Can you throw the ball against a wall and catch it before it hits the floor?
13. While throwing the ball up and catching it, can you begin moving about in space? Begin by moving slowly while throwing the ball up with only a little force. Then move faster and throw the ball up higher. Try to maintain control as you throw and catch the ball.
14. While you are throwing and catching the ball, change your direction as you move. Can you move in a forward, backward, or sideward direction as you throw and catch the ball?
15. Combine two or more space, time, or force factors while you throw and catch the ball by yourself. While moving in a sideward direction, throw the ball into the air with a weak force and catch it at a high level. How many other factors can you combine?
16. Can you throw the ball with some accuracy at a stationary target while you move in a forward, backward, or sideward direction?
17. Throw balls of different sizes and weights at targets placed at different distances away from you. Throw overhand and underhand as you attempt to hit the target. Throw in a forward direction and then in a backward direction between your legs. Throw the balls from high, medium, and low levels.
18. Repeat experiments 16 and 17 by placing the targets in a vertical plane. Draw targets on paper to place on a wall. Hang hoops at different levels from a basketball goal. Vary the distance you stand from the target as you throw the balls.
19. Can you throw the ball through or hit a moving target (a rolling tire or hoop) while you are standing still?

20. Can you move in different directions and throw the ball at a moving target (a rolling tire or hoop)?
21. Begin using an implement that you may employ to aid you in throwing and/or catching objects. Repeat all or part of activities 1 to 20 while you use a glove, plastic scoop, or cradle to assist you in your throwing and/or catching attempts. Throw the ball with your free hand and catch it with the implement. Throw and catch at different levels. Apply and receive varying amounts of force. Stay in your own space, then move about as you throw and catch objects with the aid of your implement.

Partner (Figs. 2-3 and 2-4)

1. Play catch with a partner and vary the distance from which you throw. Start rather close and gradually move farther apart. How far apart can you get and still throw and catch the ball without dropping it?
2. As you play catch with a partner, experiment by throwing and catching the ball in different ways. Throw with your right hand, left hand, overhand, underhand, sidearm, etc. Catch the ball over your head, near the ground, under your leg, to your right, to your left, etc.
3. Throw the ball in different directions as you play catch with a partner. Throw it forward, then backward under your legs like a hike in football.
4. Vary the pathway and level of the ball as you throw it to your partner. Throw it in a rather straight pathway at a medium or low level. Throw it in a vertical pathway at a high level.
5. Can you throw the ball from a low level and have your partner catch it at a medium or high level?

Fig. 2-3. Play catch cooperatively with a partner.

Fig. 2-4. Pass the ball to your partner who is on the move.

6. Can you throw the ball from a high level and have your partner catch it at a medium or low level?
7. Play catch with a partner using objects of different sizes, weights, textures, shapes, colors, etc. Vary the level, direction, and force of your throws.
8. Change the amount of force you use to throw the ball as you play catch with your partner. Throw it rather softly with a small amount of force. Throw it sharply with more force. Be careful not to throw the ball too hard.
9. Can you jump up into the air and throw the ball to your partner? Perform this activity while both of you are standing still, while the thrower is on the move and the catcher standing still, while the thrower is standing still and the catcher is on the move, and while both of you are on the move.
10. Can you throw the ball so that your partner has to jump high in the air to catch it? Perform this activity as in no. 9 with respect to no movement, one person moving, and both people moving.
11. Combine two or more space, time, or force factors at the same time as you play catch with your partner. From a medium level throw the ball with great force (hard) in a forward direction to your partner. From a low level throw (hike) the ball with a weak force in a backward direction to your partner. Think of other examples.
12. As you throw, stand still, but make your partner move to catch the ball. Make the catcher move up, back, right, and left to catch the ball.
13. Can you throw the ball while you are on the move to your partner who is standing still?
14. Can you throw and catch the ball with your partner as you are both on the move? Start slowly and then move faster.

15. Pass the ball back and forth with your partner as you move through space while changing your relationships and pathways. Move forward side by side—first near each other, then farther away. Move in a circular pathway while face to face. Can you change your relationships and direction of movement while passing the ball?
16. With a partner or a small group, progress in a forward direction downfield while passing the ball only in a backward direction. How can the ball best be thrown in this manner? (Rugby players choose a two-handed underhand toss while remaining close to teammates. Football players do the same while lateraling the ball.)
17. Play catch with a partner while using an implement to aid you in your attempts to throw and catch objects. Use gloves, plastic scoops, buckets, cradles, etc. and repeat activities 1 to 16. Throw and catch at various levels. Apply and receive varying amounts of force. Play catch while standing still and while on the move. How many different ways can you use the implements to assist your throwing and catching efforts?

ROLLING AND SLIDING ACTIVITIES THROUGH EXPLORATION AND PROBLEM SOLVING

1. Roll a ball or slide an object along a line for accuracy. Start by applying a little force and gradually apply more. How much force can you apply to the object and still keep it on the line?
2. Roll a ball or slide an object a specific distance—5, 10, and 15 feet. How much force do you need to apply to get the object to go each distance?
3. Apply as much force as you can and roll or slide an object as far as you can. Use objects of different weights, sizes, and shapes. How far can you propel each object?
4. Roll or slide an object at a target. How far away can you go from the target and still make the object hit or go through the target?
5. Stand facing a wall and roll a ball or slide another object against it. Then catch the ball as it rolls or the object as it slides back to you. Apply different amounts of force. Vary the distance you stand away from the wall. Roll the ball or slide the object directly at the wall; then project it at an angle toward the wall. Move to catch the ball or object as it comes back to you off the wall. Can you guess the angle at which the object will come back to you if you know the angle at which it was projected?
6. Stand facing a partner and play catch by rolling a ball back and forth to each other. Vary the distance you stand from your partner. Vary the amount of force you use to roll the ball. Each time you catch the ball, try to move toward it while catching it.
7. Perform the same activity as in no. 6, but this time have one partner roll the ball and the other return the ball by throwing it through the air.

8. Play catch with a partner by rolling the ball to an open space and making your partner move to catch the ball.
9. Vary the object that you roll or slide to a partner. Use big heavy balls. Use small light balls. Use plastic pucks that slide along the floor. How many types of objects can you think of within reason that could be used in games for rolling or sliding? As you roll or slide the object, can you say anything about the force required to get the object to your partner? As you catch a rolling or sliding object can you say anything about the effort it takes you to absorb the force from a moving object?

GUIDED DISCOVERY PROBLEMS FOR THROWING

1. While throwing against a wall or to a partner, stand and face the point at which you are throwing. At first throw only with your forearm by holding your elbow near your side.
2. Next, use your whole arm to throw the ball at the wall or to your partner, while continuing to face the target. Use a follow-through.
3. Now introduce a stepping action as you continue to throw. Sometimes step forward with the left foot, then the right. Which feels better? (Foot on the opposite side of the throwing arm.)
4. Now use your whole body as you throw the ball. How can you twist your body away from the target as you wind up, and toward the target as you throw the ball?
5. Finally, put steps 1 to 4 together. Use the whole arm to gain leverage. Step forward with the opposite foot to let the trunk twist and gain a good base of support. Sum up the focus from the leg, trunk, arm, and fingers to get maximum force and efficiency in your throw.
6. How far can you throw the ball? Go retrieve it and continue to see how far you can throw it. How do you use your various body parts to apply as much force as possible?
7. Try to throw the ball as far as you can again, only this time concentrate on the angle of your throw. At what angle should you throw to gain the greatest distance? What if you throw the ball straight out (0 degrees)? What happens when you throw the ball high (70 to 90 degrees)? What conclusions can you draw about the angle of the throw when trying for distance? (45 degrees.)
8. Can you aim at a target and throw for accuracy? How far can you move away from the target and still accurately hit it with your throw? How does your throw differ when you throw for accuracy? How much force do you apply?
9. Set up targets at three different distances—5, 10, and 15 feet. Use balls of three different weights—table tennis ball, tennis ball, and basketball—to throw at the targets. How much force does it take to throw balls of differ-

ent weights different distances? (It takes more force to throw heavier balls greater distances.)

10. Repeat the experiment in no. 9 but place the targets at different levels on the wall—0, 10, and 15 feet high. (It takes more force to throw balls to a higher level.)
11. Throw or pass the ball to your partner, allowing it to bounce between you. Where should the ball bounce to best enable your partner to catch it? What happens when the ball bounces near the feet of the person catching it?
12. As you bounce or pass the ball to your partner, practice putting spin on the ball. How can you put topspin on it? Backspin? How can you make the ball spin to the left or right? What happens when the ball is spinning and bounces on the ground or hits a wall? After some practice, could you come up with some statements on the reaction a spinning ball makes on its rebound? How could you use this to your advantage in sports?
13. If you are trying to throw the ball to a partner, but there is some chance that a defensive player may intercept the throw, how can you best throw the ball to avoid an interception? Under what conditions would you throw to your partner rather directly with a lot of force? (When you have a direct line to your partner with no one standing between you.) When would you try to lob the ball to your partner with a high arc and a small or medium amount of force? (When there is a defensive player between you and your partner.)
14. Try to slide a beanbag or roll a ball in a straight pathway on the floor. Choose a line or crack on the floor as your guideline. Can you accurately apply force so that the object stays on the line? Where do you have to apply force to accomplish this task? What happened in your force application if the object moved to the right or left?
15. Try to roll or slide an object a specific distance (5, 10, 15, and 20 feet). How much force should you apply to get the object to travel along the floor that specific distance? How does the force vary as you change objects that you slide or roll along the floor? (The heavier the object, the more force must be applied.) What role does friction play in the distance an object rolls or slides along the floor? Once momentum is built up, which object takes longer time or more force to stop—a heavy or a light object?
16. What is the potential value in using an implement to help you throw, roll, or slide an object (scoop in jai alai, cradle in lacrosse, cue in shuffleboard)? Practice throwing, rolling, or sliding an object for distance with and without the use of an implement. After you have gained some skill in your performance, would you say that an implement allows you to throw farther? Or does it act as a hindrance to your force application? (An implement increases leverage and mechanical advantage, thereby allowing you to throw farther.)

GUIDED DISCOVERY PROBLEMS FOR CATCHING

1. How many different body parts can you use to catch the ball? (Hands, elbows, forearm, trunk, and legs.)
2. What body parts best help you to catch the ball? (Hands.) Can you use only your hands to catch the ball?
3. Hold your hands and arms stiff when you catch the ball. Now, "give" with your arms and hands as you catch the ball. What method helps you catch the ball better? Why? (Bending or giving with the force helps absorb the force of the ball over a longer distance and a longer period of time.)
4. Try to catch a ball that has been thrown high, low, to the right, and to the left.
5. What is the position of your hands when you catch the ball above your chest? (Thumbs close together with fingers pointed up.)
6. What is the position of your hands when you catch the ball below your waist? (Little fingers close together with fingers pointed down.)
7. Can you practice these techniques as you catch the ball while standing still?
8. Can you practice these techniques as you catch the ball while moving in different directions at various speeds?
9. Can you use different kinds of implements to help you catch the ball? A plastic scoop, a tin can, a bucket, etc. What happens if you hold the implements stiffly as you attempt to catch? How can you catch most efficiently?
10. Practice moving toward and away from balls as you attempt to catch them. If it became important for you to catch a ball as soon as possible in a game, in what direction would you move to catch it? Why? (Rushing a bunt in baseball, meeting a pass in basketball.)
11. If you are going to catch a ball, but there is some chance a defensive player might intercept the throw, what can you do to enhance your chances of a successful catch? (Try to move away from the defensive player, move to an open space.)

COOPERATIVE AND COMPETITIVE GAMES

Because it is not the purpose of this book to structure teacher-designed games, the intent of the remainder of this chapter is to set a major focus, or theme, for a game. It is your role as teacher to help children learn about and play within the framework, or guidelines, for game playing, as outlined in Chapter 1. After the children have become familiar with various playing areas, field designs, open and closed games, time factors, scoring systems, strategies, penalties for rule infractions, etc., they may design their own games according to their own level of abilities and interests. Initial games tend to be cooperative in nature with a few simple rules. Later the games will involve more rules, a higher level of strategy, and competition.

■ Given a ball (yarn ball, football, tennis ball, playground ball, etc.) or another object such as a balloon or a Frisbee, make up a game with your friends (group of 4 to 6 players). Use one or more of the following rules as the focus, or theme, of your game.

Rules

1. Throw and catch the ball at a high level.
2. Pass and catch the ball at a medium level. This game may include no bounces or allowing the ball to bounce.
3. Roll or throw and catch the ball at a low level.
4. Vary the distance from which you throw and catch the ball.
5. Vary the force you apply to an object (balloon, paper airplane, Frisbee, etc.) and see how far it travels as you throw it.
6. Stress accuracy as you throw and catch the ball.
7. Throw and catch the ball while in a stationary position.
8. Throw and catch the ball while moving.
9. Throw the ball in a vertical pathway (high up in the air) and then catch it. This game may include bounces or no bounces.
10. Move side by side with a teammate as you try to travel in the playing area.
11. Throw the ball up in the air, let it bounce a specified number of times, and then catch it.
12. Throw the ball at a target marked on the wall or floor. Vary the size of the target, distance from the target, level of the target, and the style of the throw.

■ Given a ball and several hoops, make up a game with your friends. Use one or more of the following rules as the focus, or theme, of your game.

Rules

1. Place one or more hoops on the floor in a straight line and throw the ball so that it bounces once in each hoop. Vary the distance between hoops so that the amount of force you use to throw the ball has to change.
2. Suspend one or more hoops in the air in a vertical plane and try to throw the ball through the target. Vary the type of throw, level of the suspended hoop, and your distance from the hoop.
3. Suspend or hold one or more hoops in a horizontal plane and try to throw the ball through the target. Vary the type of throw, level of the suspended hoop, and your distance from the hoop.
4. Hold onto one or more hoops and move it (them) in some way (up and down, side to side, twisting) while a partner tries to throw a ball through the moving target. Vary the type of throw and your distance from the hoop.
5. Roll a hoop across the floor and try to throw a ball through the moving target.
6. Roll a hoop across the floor. While traveling with a partner along the

path of the moving hoop, see how many times you can pass the ball through the hoop.

7. Use the hoop as an area in which players must stand. Line up three hoops and perform the following activities.
   a. Have the 2 outside players throw and catch the ball while trying to keep it away from the one in the middle hoop.
   b. Have the 2 outside players throw and catch the ball while trying to hit the one in the middle below the waist with the ball. It is the objective of the middle person to dodge the ball while maintaining at least one foot in the hoop.

■ Given a ball, beanbag, deck tennis ring, Frisbee, etc. and a target such as a tire, plastic bottles, Indian clubs, wastebasket, cardboard box, etc., make up a game with your friends. Use one or more of the following rules as the focus, or theme, of your game.

Rules

1. Set up two plastic bottles, traffic cones, or Indian clubs side by side and attempt to roll, slide, or throw an object between them. Start with the targets wide apart and move them closer together. Start close to the targets and move farther away.
2. Use a tire, wastebasket, or cardboard box as a target and try to throw balls of different sizes, weights, and shapes into the targets from different distances.
3. Perform the same activity as in no. 2, except try to throw the ball into the stationary target while you are on the move.
4. Perform the same activity as in no. 2, except try to throw the ball into the target while an opponent is guarding you or the target.
5. Use a deck tennis ring or something similar to ring an Indian club, plastic bottle, or other appropriate target. Vary the size of the ring and the distance of the thrower from the target.
6. Roll or slide a ball, beanbag, or other object at a target such as plastic bottles or Indian clubs. Vary the size of the ball, size of the target, number of "pins" in the target, and the distance of the thrower from the target.

■ Given a ball and a scoop, lacrosse cradle, or glove, make up a game with your friends. Use one or more of the following rules as the focus, or theme, of your game.

Rules

1. Throw the ball with your dominant hand and catch it with the implement held in your nondominant hand. Vary the level, distance, style of throwing and catching, and force application as you make up your game.
2. Perform the same activities in no. 1, except catch with the implement held in your dominant hand and throw with the nondominant hand.

3. With either your dominant or nondominant hand throw and catch while using the implement to apply and receive force. Vary the level, distance, and style of throwing and catching.
4. Throw and/or catch a ball using a scoop while moving in different directions and pathways at different speeds and levels.
5. Change your relationship to your partner, sometimes emphasizing a face-to-face, throwing and catching pattern with the implement and at other times a side-by-side relationship.
6. Use the implement to help you throw the ball at a target or goal.
7. Repeat activities 4 to 6 with an opponent guarding you or the target.

■ Given a ball, beanbag, or other object and a geometry, alphabet, or number grid (Fig. 2-5), make up a game with your friends. Use one or more of the following rules as the focus, or theme, of your game.

Rules

1. Throw one or more beanbags for accuracy into the grid targets. Try to spell a word, hit a geometrical target, or add some numbers as the beanbags land in the grid areas.

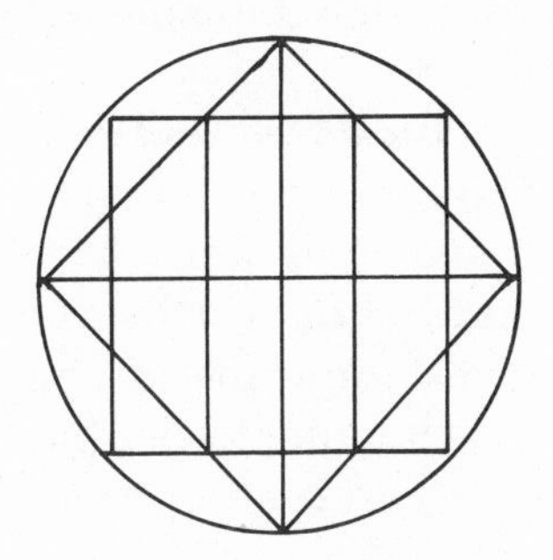

A	K	I	F	X	O
R	U	P	E	M	A
G	E	A	U	Z	H
T	Y	I	E	U	B
L	I	O	Q	O	S
C	W	N	D	V	J

1	3	7	5	0	9
0	8	6	2	4	1
5	4	+	−	0	3
2	7	= ×	÷	8	6
9	3	6	7	9	1
0	1	4	8	5	2

Fig. 2-5. Geometric, alphabet, and number grids.

2. With the alphabet grid perform the following activities while standing across from a partner:
   a. Bounce-pass the ball into consecutive letters of the alphabet (A, B, C . . .). As your partner catches the ball, he must locate the next successive letter and bounce-pass it back to you through that letter.
   b. Spell words as you bounce-pass the ball back and forth with your partner.
3. With the number grid perform the following activities while standing across from a partner:
   a. Bounce-pass the ball into consecutive numbers (0, 1, 2 . . .). As your partner catches the ball, he must locate the next successive number and bounce it back to you through that number.
   b. Perform mathematics operations (add, subtract, multiply, divide) as you bounce-pass the ball back and forth with a partner. The first thrower bounce-passes the ball into a number (3) and calls out an operation (add). The partner throws the ball into a different number (2) and calls out a different operation (equals). The first thrower must throw the ball into the answer.
4. With the geometry grid perform the following activities while standing across from a partner:
   a. Call out a geometrical form and then try to bounce-pass the ball into that form as you throw the ball to your partner.
   b. Have a leader and a follower. The leader may bounce-pass the ball into any geometrical form as he throws it to the follower (partner). The follower must throw the ball into the same geometrical form as he returns the ball to the leader (partner).

SAMPLE GAMES

GAME 1

Major focus: Roll a ball at a low level in an attempt to hit a target.
Number of players: 2.
Equipment: A ball and four to six pins or plastic bottles.
Playing area: A rectangular area (line formation) 6 × 15 feet (Fig. 2-6).
Attempts: Two tries from each distance.
Rules: Each player makes two attempts to roll the ball from each distance. The objective is to knock over all six pins.
Scoring

At 5 feet			
All pins on first try	4 points +	5-point bonus =	9 points
All pins after two tries	4 points	2-point bonus	7 points
3 pins	3 points		3 points
2 pins	2 points		2 points
1 pin	1 point		1 point
At 10 feet			
All pins on first try	4 points +	10-point bonus =	14 points
All pins after two tries	4 points	5-point bonus	9 points
3 pins	6 points		6 points
2 pins	4 points		4 points
1 pin	2 points		2 points
At 15 feet			
All pins on first try	4 points +	15-point bonus =	19 points
All pins after two tries	4 points	10-point bonus	14 points
3 pins	9 points		9 points
2 pins	6 points		6 points
1 pin	3 points		3 points

Fouls and penalties: If a player steps over the line on any attempt, he loses his turn.

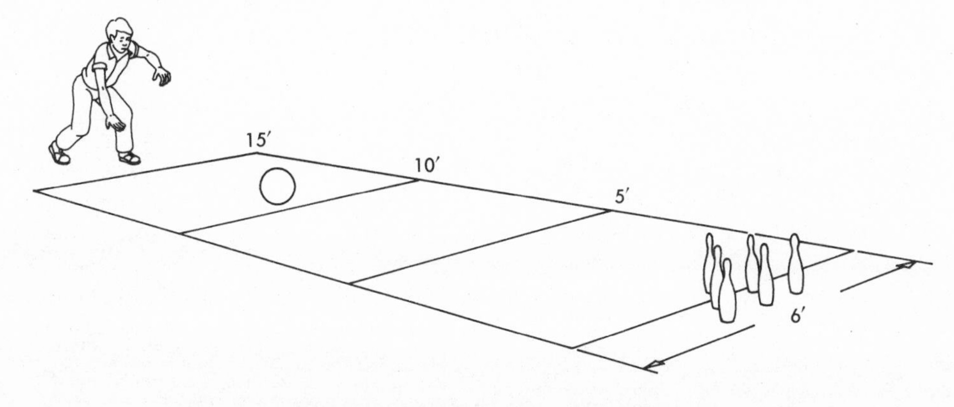

Fig. 2-6. Roll the ball at a low level.

GAME 2

Major focus: Throw the ball through targets placed at different levels and in different planes.

Number of players: 4.

Equipment: A ball and two hoops.

Playing area: A rectangular area 6 × 30 feet (Fig. 2-7).

Attempts: Four tries.

Rules: Each player makes four attempts to throw the ball from each distance. The objective is to throw the ball so that it passes through both hoops, one placed in a vertical plane and the other in a horizontal plane. Players take turns throwing and holding the hoops. Players may throw the ball underhand or overhand.

Scoring

At 5 feet
- Both hoops 5 points
- One hoop 2 points

At 10 feet
- Both hoops 10 points
- One hoop 4 points

At 15 feet
- Both hoops 15 points
- One hoop 6 points

Fouls and penalties: No player holding a hoop may move it to distract the thrower during any attempt. Any such infraction results in an opportunity for the thrower to make another try.

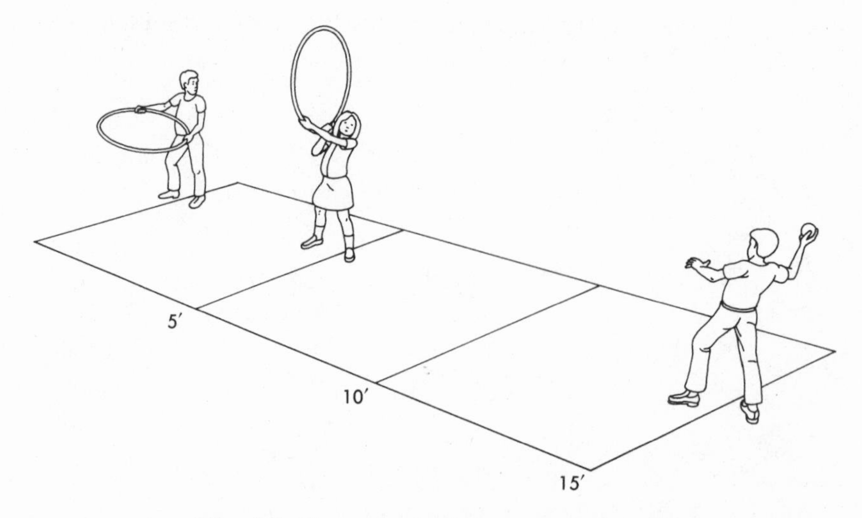

Fig. 2-7. Throw the ball through the hoops.

GAME 3

Major focus: Throw and catch the ball at a high level.
Number of players: 4.
Equipment: A ball and a net.
Playing area: A rectangular area 10 × 20 feet with a net or a rope through the middle at a 6-foot height (a net game) (Fig. 2-8).
Rules: With 2 teammates standing on the same side of the net in a 10 × 10 foot area, the objective of the game is to throw and catch the ball at a high level over the net. Balls must be thrown and caught above chest level. After an initial throw the ball is thrown and caught on alternate sides until a point is scored. Balls must be thrown with some arc, but no spiking is allowed. Only the team that has the serve may score a point. Catchers may hold the ball for no more than 3 seconds before making a throw to their teammate or over the net to their opponents. There may be one throw to a teammate before the ball must be thrown over the net.
Scoring: One point is scored when—

1. The serving team places the ball in the opponents' court so that it is not caught.
2. The receiving team catches the ball below the chest.
3. The receiving team throws the ball out-of-bounds.

A side out is scored when—

1. The serving team throws the ball out-of-bounds.
2. The receiving team places the ball in the opponents' court so that it cannot be caught.
3. The serving team catches the ball below the chest.

Ten points constitute a game.
Fouls and penalties: The following infractions result in a point or a side out, depending on whether the serving or receiving team commits the foul:

1. Spiking the ball.
2. Throwing the ball with no arc.
3. Throwing the ball into or under the net.
4. Any player going under, into, or over the net to play a ball.

Fig. 2-8. Throw and catch the ball over the net.

GAME 4

Major focus: Throw the ball at a target by using different styles of throws and balls of various sizes, weights, and shapes.

Number of players: 2 to 4.

Equipment: Two boxes, two Hula-Hoops or ropes, and various types of balls.

Playing area: An area approximately 5 × 20 feet (Fig. 2-9).

Rules: As in horseshoes, players take turns throwing (two balls per turn) at the targets. The game may be played as singles or doubles. Various rounds may stipulate types of throws or various balls.

Scoring: A ball landing in the box counts 5 points. A ball landing in the hoop or rope counts 3 points. A game is comprised of 50 points.

Fouls: Players must throw from behind their target. A player throwing from in front of the target loses his turn.

Fig. 2-9. Throw the ball into the box or ring.

GAME 5

Major focus: Throw for accuracy at a target by using different styles of throws and balls of various sizes, weights, and shapes. Horseshoes and/or Frisbees* may be used.

Number of players: 2.

Equipment: A wastebasket and/or a cardboard box and five different types of balls such as a football, tennis ball, table tennis ball, yarn ball, and playground ball; or horseshoes and/or Frisbees.

Playing area: A circular area with a 15-foot radius (Fig. 2-10).

Rules: Starting at a distance of 5 feet from the center target, each player makes five attempts to throw five different objects into or near the target. The first thrower chooses a particular style of throwing (overhand, underhand, right hand, left hand, backward between the legs, etc.), which must also be used during the partner's turn. Each set of turns involves the selection of a new style of throwing. After running out of styles of throwing, the players may move farther away from the target and repeat the sequence.

Scoring: One point for each ball, horseshoe, or Frisbee thrown into or nearest the target, with a maximum of 5 points for each turn.

Fouls and penalties: Failure to use the required style of throwing or stepping over the restraining line results in loss of turn.

---

*For a variety of Frisbee games the reader is referred to Johnson (1975).

Fig. 2-10. Throw the ball into the target.

GAME 6

Major focus: Throw and catch the ball while moving around in space. To free themselves to catch the ball, players must move to an open space.

Number of players: 6.

Equipment: A ball.

Playing area: A rectangular area 20 × 60 feet (a field game) (Fig. 2-11).

Rules: The objective is for the 3 offensive players to advance the ball downcourt in an attempt to score a goal. Players must pass and catch the ball. They may not hold the ball for more than 3 seconds. They may not take more than three running steps while they possess the ball, although they may run anywhere in an effort to get clear (Fig. 2-10). Two defensive players guard the 3 offensive players while 1 defensive player guards the goal. Throws at the goal must be made from behind the 15-foot perimeter area. Any ball that goes out-of-bounds on the sidelines goes to the team that was last in possession. Teams take turns on offense and defense, each turn starting at one end line and finishing with a throw at the goal. Any interception of a pass by a defensive player while the ball is in play ends the offensive set.

Scoring: One point is scored for each successful goal. One game is composed of 10 points.

Fouls and penalties: The following infractions result in a side out or the opposing team getting the ball:

1. Holding the ball for more than 3 seconds.
2. Taking more than three steps with the ball.
3. Being inside the perimeter area on a goal attempt.

The following infraction results in a free throw at the goal, with only the goal keeper guarding the area:

1. Holding, blocking, tripping, or preventing an offensive player from free movement.

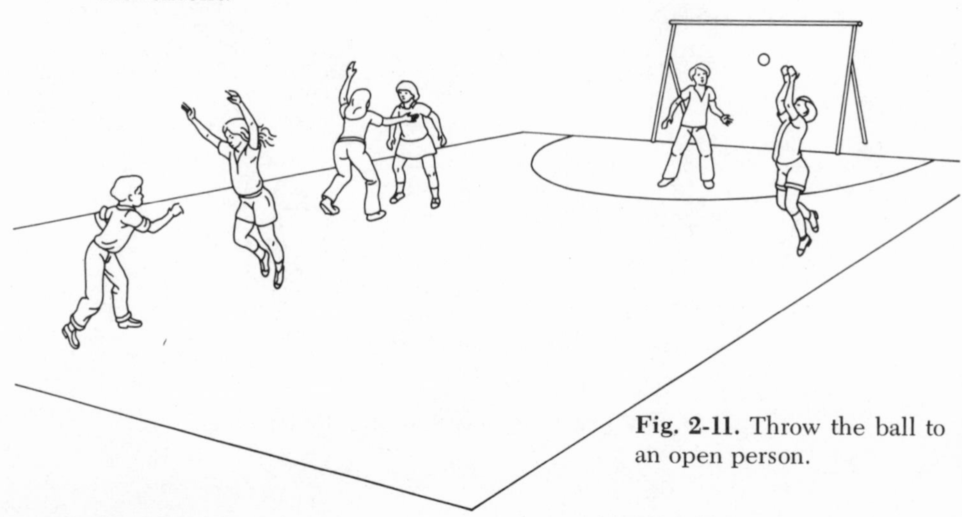

Fig. 2-11. Throw the ball to an open person.

GAME 7

Major focus: As a group the team must cooperatively throw the ball over the net and catch it as it is returned to them.

Number of players: 4 to 20.

Equipment: A volleyball or badminton net and standards, a cage ball or other type of large ball, and two towels, sheets, or blankets.

Playing area: A rectangular area approximately 30 × 60 feet (Fig. 2-12).

Rules: Players on each team must work together to cooperatively throw and catch the ball over the net. If there are 2 players per team, towels are used. Larger groups may use sheets or blankets.

Scoring: Each team starts with 10 points. The serving team is designated by a coin toss. One point is taken away each time a team successfully throws the ball into their opponents' court and it touches the ground. Only the serving team may have points reduced from their score. When a team reaches zero (0 points) the teams change members and a new game is started.

Fouls and penalties: If the ball is thrown out-of-bounds, a loss of serve occurs, and/or 1 point is added to the score.

Fig. 2-12. Cooperate with a partner to throw the ball over the net.

GAME 8

Major focus: Throw an object for combined distance and accuracy in an effort to reach a target in the least number of throws possible.

Number of players: 1 to 20.

Equipment: A ball or Frisbee, as well as some plastic bottles, hoops, or tires for targets. Brooms and traffic cones may also be the "holes."

Playing area: A large open space that may have trees, shrubs, or water for hazards.

Rules: The rules for this game are the same as for golf, except the ball or Frisbee is thrown rather than struck. The objective is to start at the tee and throw the ball or Frisbee the least number of times while trying to get it to land in the target. Some holes may be short, some may be long. Some hazards may be a road, sidewalk, shrub, ditch, etc. Any ball or Frisbee landing in a hazard area is out-of-bounds, and a penalty stroke must be taken. Trees or buildings provide interesting layouts for the course by furnishing doglegs and rough areas.

Scoring: One point for each throw. Match play or the lowest score may be used in determining winners.

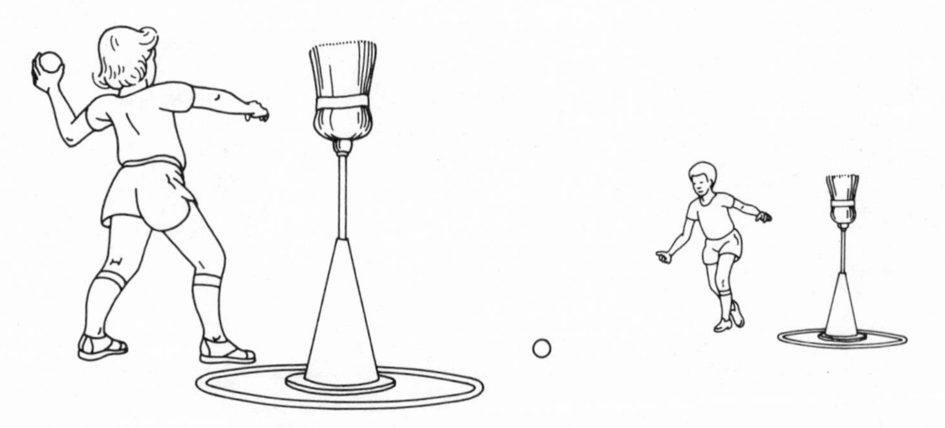

Fig. 2-13. Throw the object to the "flag."

CHAPTER THREE

Kicking and trapping

It is a historical fact that in the United States more attention is paid to games requiring use of the hands and arms as primary manipulative agents rather than the feet and legs. Games of kicking and trapping are characterized by use of the lower part of the body to control the ball. Games of this type are challenging but sometimes frustrating to the child because of a lack of development of the body parts used to propel the ball away from the body and/or receive the force of the ball as it comes toward the body. Through careful planning and consideration of some of the principles of human development, it is possible to develop sets of experiences in which children become nearly as skillful with their feet and legs as they are with their hands and arms. With the advent of soccer as a major sport in the United States, it will become increasingly more important to provide these experiences.

PRINCIPLES OF HUMAN DEVELOPMENT

Just as the throwing and catching patterns evolve from reflex actions to those of prehension, the kicking and trapping patterns may be compared to the walking reflex and initial attempts at walking and running. However, because actual walking or running patterns develop at a later stage than does prehension, one could expect a delayed development in kicking skill. To effectively kick or trap a ball well, a person must be able to balance while standing on one leg in an effort to control the ball effectively with the free leg.

Other factors also enter the picture. Child development progresses from head to toe (cephalocaudal), from flexion to extension, from proximal to distal, and from unilateral to contralateral movements. Because the lower part of the body develops last, teachers should take great care in providing children with concentrated manipulative experiences for the feet and legs. At times bare feet and legs would allow children to become sensitive to the size, texture, shape, and force of various balls. To ensure proper posture while kicking, the postural or labyrinthine (flexion-extension) reflexes must be overcome. It requires a voluntary motor act to extend at the knees and flex at the hips while keeping the back and head in proper alignment. Because the large muscles of the trunk and leg develop before the small muscles of the foot, teachers should expect general form to precede any refined movements that require fine manipulative control, such as changes in direction, force application, speed, and pathway. In initial attempts at kicking and trapping, a child tends to use predominantly one side of the body. Gradually, the child will change over to a more mature form in which the arm on the side opposite the kicking or trapping leg is held out or extended for balance purposes.

Principles of visual perception affect a child's kicking and trapping abilities, just as they influence a child's throwing and catching. Initial farsightedness hinders a child's ability to focus on an object as he prepares to kick or trap it. The eye-foot coordination required to kick or trap a moving ball develops gradually during the elementary school years until at 11 or 12 years of age a child can finally reliably kick or trap a ball while he himself is on the move. Visual figure-ground perception also plays an important role in the development of kicking and trapping. A ball that provides a good color contrast with the floor, grass, dirt, etc. should be used so that children can see it well.

KICKING

As stated previously in Chapter 1, kicking is one of a variety of striking actions executed by the body. During the execution of a kick, the leg builds up momentum prior to making contact with the ball. At the point of momentary contact, maximum force is applied to the ball with the foot.

Regardless of the style of kick, there seem to be three stages through which children pass on their way to a mature kicking pattern. By the time a child is 2 years old he has developed enough balance control to stand on one foot and kick with the other. During this *initial* stage the child's leg action is limited in the backswing, or preparatory, phase of the kick. The forward kicking motion

Fig. 3-1. Children learn to kick balls in developmental stages.

itself is short, with little or no follow-through. The leg kicks *at* the ball rather than "through" it. The action of the arms and trunk during the kick is limited because the body is held erect, with the arms held either at the sides or outward for stability. Despite the child's early kicking capability, performance is extremely unpredictable. His performance could vary from running against the ball to nudging or pushing it, or even to missing it.

During the second, or *elementary,* stage of development the major change in the kicking process is in the preparatory phase. There is a definite flexion of the kicking leg prior to the act of kicking. (See Fig. 3-1.) By age 6 most children are capable of performing at a mature level while kicking. At the third, or *mature,* stage they have learned that forward motion prior to the kick is important. The preparatory phase is initiated at the hip, with less flexion at the knee. The kicking leg swings through a long arc and kicks through the ball rather than at it. The follow-through with the leg is complete as the trunk leans forward toward the ball and the arms are used for balance. The arms and feet act in opposition, as in the throwing action.

Just as in throwing, there are several varieties of kicking. A person may kick the ball from a stationary position, as in the kickoff or field goal in football. In this type of kick the approach may be in a forward direction, with the toe applying the force, or from the side, with the forepart of the instep applying the force. A person may kick the ball while on the move with various parts of the foot, as in soccer. This type of kick often requires the player to kick equally well with either foot. The force may be applied by the toe, inside or outside of the foot, or even the heel. Various amounts of force are applied, depending on the distance of the intended kick. The kicker must learn to stop, start, and change directions quickly. The punt is perhaps the most difficult of all kicks to learn because it requires a complex coordination of body movements. The kicker must move his body forward, drop a held ball accurately, and kick it with the foot before it touches the ground. Because of the difficulty in timing, skill in punting is not expected until a child is 5 or 6 years old.

As children learn to kick by using the different styles, their experiences should be varied in an attempt to develop a pattern that is adaptable in many game situations. Children should begin with lightweight balls of a medium to large size and learn to kick other balls of differents sizes, shapes, textures, and weights. Playground balls, yarn balls, rugby balls, soccer balls, footballs, etc. should be used in an appropriate manner to help children learn to kick for form, accuracy, and distance. Children should be given the opportunity to kick from stationary positions, as well as while on the move. They should kick in different directions and also vary the trajectory of the ball as they change the force and the speed with which force is applied. It is also important in different games to be able to kick the ball equally well with either foot.

TRAPPING

As a skill, trapping may be defined as the process of receiving, or absorbing, the force of a moving object (usually a ball) with the lower part of the body. Generally the feet are used to gain control of a moving ball or stop it, although the shins, thighs, and abdomen can be used effectively for the same purpose. The skill is employed in ball games in which the hands may not be used (soccer) to gain control of the ball so that the player can prepare to travel with it or kick it away.

Unlike kicking, throwing, or catching, the skill of trapping has stimulated little, if any, motor development research. Perhaps the reason is that the sport of soccer has not become popular in the United States. With current trends giving this sport more exposure to today's boys and girls, it is hoped that this fact will change. Children seem to pass through three stages in learning the skill of trapping, although research does not support this description.

In the *initial* stage, attempts at trapping a ball are rather passive, since there is no real attempt to absorb the force of the ball while maintaining control. Either the child is standing in one place while the moving ball bounces off his shins, or he makes an attempt to put one foot on top of the moving ball, bringing it to an abrupt stop. Care has to be taken to make sure the child does not try to stand on the ball with one foot, since he may lose his balance and fall. Because the ball sometimes actually rebounds off the child's body due to poor timing, he may acquire an avoidance reaction. The use of a soft or somewhat deflated ball may help the child gain more success and feel more confident.

Fig. 3-2. Trap the ball with different body parts.

During the second, or *elementary,* stage of trapping the child becomes aware of the concept of absorbing force. A definite attempt is made to "give with the ball" or receive the ball with respect to time, space, and force. He may try to trap the ball by reducing its force with different parts of the body. One example is between the foot and the ground (Fig. 3-2). If the ball is bouncing, he may trap it between the ground and the shin or between the top part of the foot and the shin at the ankle. If the ball is higher in the air, he may try to stop it by trapping it with his abdomen, bending at the hips. Children have their best control while remaining in a stationary position, but they should begin trying to trap the ball while on the move.

In the third, or *mature,* stage a child is able to effectively use his trapping skills while both he and the ball are on the move. To ensure flexibility of movement response, balls of different sizes traveling with different amounts of force from various directions should be trapped. Children should learn to trap the ball equally well with both sides of the body (left-right).

KICKING AND TRAPPING ACTIVITIES THROUGH EXPLORATION AND PROBLEM SOLVING

Individual

1. Get a ball and move to your own space. With just a little force, kick it a short distance. Watch how far it rolls. Kick it again with the same amount of force. Run after it and see if you can trap it before the rolling ball comes to a stop.
2. See how far you can kick the ball. Vary your style of kicking. Which style allows you to kick the ball the farthest?

3. See how high you can kick the ball. Vary your style of kicking. Can you kick the ball higher with a kickoff or a punt style?
4. Can you travel and kick the ball so that it stays close to your body? On a signal stop and trap the ball.
5. When traveling with the ball, can you alternate feet while kicking? When you are ready, try to trap the ball. Also, when you feel you are about to lose control of the ball, try to trap it.
6. Change your speed as you move around while kicking the ball. Move slow at first and increase your speed.
7. Change your direction as you move around while kicking and trapping the ball. Move in forward, backward, and sideward directions.
8. Can you kick the ball toward a wall and trap it as it rebounds off the wall? Change the foot with which you kick. Change your style of kicking. Take turns trapping the ball with each leg.
9. While working with the ball against a wall, experiment by kicking with different degrees of force. Can you work with weak, medium, and strong forces and still trap the ball as it rebounds off the wall?
10. Practice by using different parts of your leg to trap the ball as it rebounds off the wall with varying amounts of force.
11. If the ball is traveling at a high level, can you slow it down so that it drops to the ground to be trapped? The head or chest can be used for high bounces, the legs for low bounces.
12. Vary your distance from the wall as you kick the ball against it. Can you kick the ball so that it stops before it returns to you? Can you kick it so that it stops at your feet? Can you kick it so that it rebounds past you? How does the force of your kick vary with your distance from the wall?
13. Use a milk bottle, plastic bottle, or tire as a target. Kick your ball at the target from varying distances. How far can you get away from the target and hit it? Vary your style of kicking as you continue to attempt to hit the target.
14. Can you kick the ball through a moving target (a rolling tire or hoop) while you are standing still?
15. Can you move in different directions and kick the ball at a moving target?
16. Can you kick the ball several times in succession without letting the ball touch the ground? How may this be accomplished? (Use a little force and kick directly underneath the ball.)

Partner

1. Kick and trap the ball between you and your partner. Start rather close and gradually move farther apart. How far apart can you go and still kick and trap the ball under control?
2. Practice kicking and trapping with different body parts and with different

styles. Be sure you trap the ball that your partner kicks and return it by kicking it.
3. Kick the ball with varying degrees of force while working with your partner.
4. Kick the ball in different directions, forcing your partner to move to trap the ball while it is still rolling.
5. Practice trapping and kicking the ball while both you and your partner are continuously on the move. Vary the speed with which you travel, the distance from your partner, and the force of your kicks.
6. Vary the size, weight, shape, texture, and color of the balls you and your partner kick as you perform activities 1 to 5. Which balls are most effective for different purposes?
7. Combine two or more space, time, or force factors as you kick and trap the ball with your partner. Kick the ball with a small amount of force into a medium level. Have your partner absorb the force of the ball off the chest and trap the ball in front of the body. While traveling at a fast speed down the field at a close distance to your partner, use a small amount of force to kick and trap the ball between you two. Think of other examples.
8. Can you and your partner kick the ball back and forth while taking turns kicking it at a target (carton, hoop, tire, etc.)?

GUIDED DISCOVERY PROBLEMS FOR KICKING

1. While kicking against a wall or to a partner, stand and face the point to which you are kicking. At first kick as follows: stand still, balance on one leg with the ball just in front of your kicking leg, and bend the kicking leg at the knee. How far does the ball go?
2. Next, use your whole leg to kick the ball at the wall or to your partner. Bend your leg at the hip and knee as you prepare to kick the ball. Use a follow-through, raising your kicking leg high after contacting the ball. Does the ball go farther when you kick it this way? Why? (Yes, you are using more body parts, which help you apply more force.)
3. Now take some steps as you move toward the ball before kicking it. Can you kick even farther now? Why? (You have developed more body momentum before your kick.)
4. When you kick be aware of what your head, trunk, and arms are doing. What about your head? (It is down, looking at the ball.) Your trunk? (It is bent a little, leaning into the ball.) Your arms? (They are held a little out to the side for balance. If you kick with your right foot, your left arm swings forward a little for better balance.)
5. With what different parts of your foot can you kick a ball placed on the floor or ground? (With the toes, the inside of the foot, the outside of the foot, and the heel.) (See Fig. 3-3.)

Fig. 3-3. Kick the ball with different parts of the foot.

6. Are you using both feet to practice your kicking? If you have a favorite, or dominant, foot with which to kick, can you use the other foot also? Can you alternate feet as you kick the ball soft? Hard?
7. If you want the ball to remain close to you as you travel down the field or through a traffic cone obstacle course, how can you best kick the ball? (Use a little force, keep the ball rolling on the ground, and for each new change of direction, kick the ball on the side opposite the line of travel.)
8. To change the direction of a moving ball, where must you kick it? (On the side opposite the line of travel. If you want the ball to travel to the left, you must kick to the right of the ball. This is an example of Newton's first (inertia) and third (action-reaction) laws of motion.)
9. If you want to kick the ball for distance with great force, which parts of your foot would you choose? You might choose your toes and approach the ball as you would a kickoff in football. You might approach the ball at an angle and kick with the inside of your foot, like a soccer-style kicker. Practice both ways. Which works best for you?
10. If you want to control the ball, keep it near you by using little force, and change directions quickly, what parts of your foot might you use to kick the ball? (The toes, inside or outside of the foot, or the heel, depending on the direction you want the ball to travel.)
11. Can you aim at a target (a milk carton, tire, or plastic bottle) and kick for accuracy? Which part of your foot could best be used for accurate kicks? (For best distance and accuracy the inside of the foot provides the flattest surface for kicking. The toes and/or shoes are pointed and may send the

ball off at inaccurate angles.) How does your kick differ when you kick for accuracy and distance? (You use less force when you kick for accuracy.)

12. If you want the ball to travel along the ground, where should you apply the force as you kick it? (In the middle, or fat, part of the ball.)
13. If you want the ball to travel into the air, where should you apply the force as you kick it? (At the bottom of the ball near the ground.)
14. To make your ball travel the greatest distance, how and when should you kick it? (By using a kickoff or soccer-style kick and applying great force, you should be able to kick the ball into the air at a 45-degree angle.)
15. Set up targets at three different distances (10, 20, and 30 feet). Use balls of four different weights (your ball, playground ball, soccer ball, rugby ball) to kick at the targets. How much force does it take to kick balls of different weights different distances? (It takes more force to kick heavier balls greater distances.)
16. Try to kick a ball so that it rolls a specific distance (10, 20, and 30 feet). Use balls of four different weights (yarn ball, playground ball, soccer ball, rugby ball) to kick. How much force should you apply to get the ball to travel along the floor that specific distance? How does the force of your kick vary as you change the object that you kick along the floor? (The heavier the object, the more force must be applied.) What role does friction play in the distance an object rolls along the floor? Once momentum is built up, which object takes longer or more force to stop—a heavy or a light one?
17. Most of the balls for kicking are round, but some are oblong. Why do you suppose they are shaped that way? Kick some balls of different shapes and notice the way they travel. A round ball always spins. An oblong ball travels end over end or it spirals. Where would you apply the force to make an oblong ball travel end over end? To get it to spiral?
18. You usually kick the ball while it is on the ground, but sometimes you kick it while it is in the air. Can you hold the ball, drop it, and kick it before it hits the ground? How should you hold the ball and then drop it to best kick it? Can you move forward as you kick the ball in the air? Can you make an oblong ball spiral as you kick (punt) it?
19. If you are trying to kick the ball to a partner, but there is some chance that a defensive player may intercept the kick, how can you best kick the ball to avoid an interception? (If the defensive player stays between you and your partner or guards nearer your partner, keep the ball and dribble down the field by yourself. If the defensive player comes to guard you closely, kick the ball to your partner with a lead pass.)

GUIDED DISCOVERY PROBLEMS FOR TRAPPING

1. How many different ways can you trap the ball with your legs?
2. What body parts are used to trap the ball? Can you demonstrate?

3. Some body parts are easier to use to trap the ball than others. Which are the easiest for you? Why?
4. Can you use your foot to trap the ball? Now, try using the other foot. Is one foot easier than the other?
5. Can you trap the ball between your shin or knee and the ground? How effective is your shin or knee when trapping the ball? Are you able to trap it with either knee or shin?
6. Concentrate on what you do with your body to bring the ball under control as you trap it. If you keep your leg rather stiff, the ball is likely to bounce out of control. If you can absorb the force of the ball by bending at the hip, knee, and/or ankle joints as it contacts your leg, the ball will stay close to you.
7. Travel and dribble a moving ball. On the signal to stop, can you trap it? Are you able to keep control of your body and the ball? Can you trap the ball with your knee, shin, or foot? Can you use either leg to trap a moving ball?
8. While traveling, can you stop and trap the ball and change directions before traveling again?
9. Can you continue to practice your trapping techniques while moving in different directions at various speeds?
10. How would you trap a ball that is bouncing or traveling through the air prior to landing? (You would still attempt to absorb the force of the ball by giving with it, but you might have to use your thighs or abdomen.)
11. If it became important for you to trap a ball as soon as possible in a game, in what direction would you move to trap it? Why? Practice moving toward and away from balls as you attempt to trap them. Remember that time and speed are important factors in gaining control of the ball.
12. If you are going to trap a ball, but there is some chance a defensive player might intercept the kick, what can you do to enhance your chances of a successful trap? (Try to move away from the defensive player. Move to an open space or toward the ball so as to place your body between the ball and the defensive player.)
13. What shape balls are used in various kicking and trapping games? (Some are round and some are oblong.)
14. Try trapping balls of different shapes. Is it more difficult to trap a round or oblong ball? Why? (A round ball is easier to trap because it travels, rolls, or bounces in a predictable pathway. An oblong ball is more difficult because it travels in unpredictable pathways while rolling or bouncing.)
15. Which games use a round ball? An oblong ball? Why?

COOPERATIVE AND COMPETITIVE GAMES

As in Chapter 2, the intent of the remainder of this chapter is to set a major focus, or theme, for purposes of stimulating games between and among children. It is your role as teacher to help children learn about and play within the framework, or guidelines, for game playing, as outlined in Chapter 1. After the children have become familiar with various playing areas, field designs, open and closed games, time factors, scoring systems, strategies, penalties for rule infractions, etc., they may design their own games according to their own level of abilities and interests. Initial games tend to be cooperative in nature with a few simple rules. Later the games will involve more rules, a higher level of strategy, and competition.

■ Given a ball (yarn ball, beach ball, playground ball, football, soccer ball, etc.) or another object such as a balloon, make up a game with your partners (a group of 2 to 6 players). Use one or more of the following rules as the focus, or theme, of your game.

Rules

1. Kick and trap the ball among the players of the game. Make sure that everyone gets a chance to touch the ball.
2. Kick and trap the ball while all players are moving.
3. Stress partner relationships in your game. Can you be face to face, side by side, near or far from other players?
4. Make up a game to determine how far you can kick the ball.
5. With a target determine how accurately you can kick the ball. Vary your distance from the target.
6. Make up a game to determine how high you can kick the ball.

■ Given a ball and some other objects such as hoops, cartons, tires, or plastic bottles, make up a game with your partners. Use one or more of the following rules as the focus, or theme, of your game.

Rules

1. Develop a kicking and trapping game that requires all players to remain inside the hoop.
2. Suspend or hold a Hula-Hoop in a vertical plane and try to kick the ball through it. Vary your distance from the target.
3. Roll a hoop across the floor and try to kick a ball through a moving target. You may kick from a stationary position or while moving with the target.
4. Set up two hoops about 15 feet apart. Have one player or team try to maneuver a ball through the hoop while the other player or team tries to do the same. If there is more than 1 player per team, all must touch the ball before it goes through the hoop. You may want to have goalies defend the hoop.
5. Kick a ball at various distances from the hoop and attempt to make it stop inside the hoop.
6. With two balls and two or more cartons set apart from each other, race your partner around, between, or among the cartons.

7. Design a game that stresses accuracy: attempt to kick balls at milk carton or plastic bottle targets from various distances. You may want to have goalies defend the targets.
8. Use hoops as an area in which players must stand. Line up three hoops and perform the following activities:
   a. Have the 2 outside players kick and trap the ball while trying to keep it away from the player in the middle hoop.
   b. Have the 2 outside players kick and trap the ball while trying to hit the middle player below the waist with the ball. It is the objective of the middle player to dodge the ball while keeping at least one foot in the hoop.

■ Given a ball and two or more scooters, make up a game with other players that uses one or more of the following rules as the central focus, or theme.

Rules

1. While sitting on the scooters, kick and trap the ball among the players. Make sure that everyone has a chance to touch the ball.
2. While moving on the scooters, kick and trap the ball among the players.
3. Kick the ball at a target or through a goal while sitting or moving on the scooters.

SAMPLE GAMES

GAME 1

Major focus: By changing force, speed, or direction, kick the ball at a low level against a wall so that the opponent cannot trap it.

Number of players: 2 to 4.

Equipment: A ball and a wall.

Playing area: An area 10 × 15 feet near a wall (Fig. 3-4).

Attempts: Each team gets ten tries to kick the ball against the wall.

Rules: The offensive team may move around behind the restraining line, which is 10 feet from the wall. They may pass (kick) the ball to a teammate. After moving around and gaining an advantageous position, any offensive player may make an attempt to kick the ball against the wall. Defensive players move around and try to trap the ball before it hits the wall.

Scoring: One point is scored for each successful attempt at hitting the wall. Defensive players score 1 point for each successful trap.

Fouls and penalties: Offensive players may not kick from inside the restraining line and may not send the ball higher than waist level. Defensive players may not trap the ball with their hands. Any infraction causes a loss of turn and scores 1 point for the opposing team.

Fig. 3-4. Kick the ball to the wall.

GAME 2

Major focus: Kick a ball over or through a target from different distances.

Number of players: 2 to 6.

Equipment: Two folding chairs, wands, rope, high jump standards, etc. and some balls.

Playing area: A rectangular area 10 × 20 feet.

Attempts: Kick the ball three times from each distance.

Rules: Each player has three turns to attempt to kick the ball over or through the goal from each distance. The goalposts are placed 6 feet apart with a crossbar 4 feet high. (See Fig. 3-5.)

Scoring: A player receives 3 points for each ball kicked through the goal and 5 points for each ball kicked over the goal. Players keep their own score. The final score is the cumulative point value from each distance.

Fouls and penalties: If a player steps over the kicking line, a loss of turn occurs.

Fig. 3-5. Kick the ball over the target.

GAME 3

Major focus: Trap the ball and prevent a point from being scored.
Number of players: 4.
Equipment: A ball and a roll of masking tape.
Playing area: A rectangular area 5 × 20 feet with a 5 × 5 foot trapping box clearly marked at one or both ends (Fig. 3-6).
Rules: As in the game of horseshoes, 1 player from each team is on each end of the court. The kicking player attempts to kick the ball down the lane. The trapping player must attempt to trap the ball as it enters the trapping box.
Scoring: One point is scored for each ball successfully trapped inside the box. A ball trapped outside the box results in no score. After 10 points, kickers and trappers switch roles.
Fouls and penalties: Any ball that is kicked outside the lane results in a rekick. The trapper must have a fair chance to control the ball within the designated area. A point is taken away from a team's score if the ball travels higher than knee level.

Fig. 3-6. Trap the ball before it reaches the end line.

GAME 4

Major focus: Kick the ball to as high a level as you can and trap it as soon as you can after it rebounds off the wall.

Number of players: 2 to 4.

Equipment: One ball for each child or a variety of different balls.

Playing area: A rectangular area near a wall approximately 20 × 60 feet (Fig. 3-7).

Rules: Each player initiates the game by making three kicks at the wall from a distance of 20 feet. The objective is for the kickers to kick each ball as high on the wall as possible and then to run and position their body in such a way as to trap the ball as quickly as possible as it rebounds off the wall. Because the ball rebounds at a high level, children have to use the trunk to make contact with the ball. Then, after letting the ball bounce to the floor (ground), they trap it with their feet. After three tries from 20 feet, the children make three attempts from 25 and 30 feet. After one round the size or type of ball may be changed and the game started over again.

Scoring: Children get two scores for each attempt. One score comes from the height of the kick, as follows:

0 to 5 feet high	1 point
5 to 10	3 points
10 to 15	5 points
Over 15	7 points

The second score comes from the trapping performance, as follows:

0 to 20 feet from wall	7 points
20 to 30	5 points
30 to 40	3 points
40 to 50	1 point
Over 50	0 points at each distance

Fouls and penalties: Kicking from in front of a particular line results in a loss of score for that attempt. Use of the hands or arms in trapping results in a loss of score for that attempt.

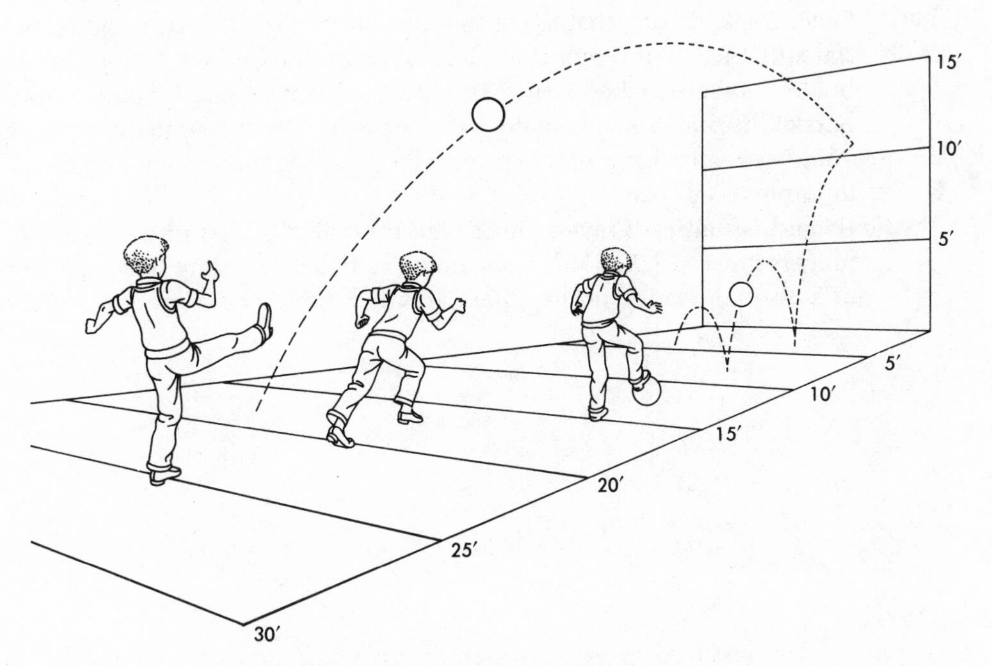

Fig. 3-7. Trap the ball as quickly as you can.

GAME 5

Major focus: Kick the ball at a target in an attempt to knock it over. Work as a team in an effort to cooperatively knock over all targets.

Number of players: 6 to 10.

Equipment: Eight to twelve targets such as bowling pins, milk cartons, or plastic bottles and from one to five balls.

Playing area: A circle with a diameter of 30 to 50 feet (Fig. 3-8).

Rules: Players must kick the balls at a low level at the targets in an effort to knock over all of them. The team must cooperatively work together to kick and knock over all the targets because they are working against a time factor. Kicked balls that are in the middle of the circle may be retrieved. Balls that travel through the circle must be trapped on the opposite side before they are kicked again. To ensure maximum participation, all members of the team must kick the ball at least two times for the turn to count.

Scoring: Scores are kept in time by seconds. Each team competes against itself to improve its score.

Fouls and penalties: Players must kick the ball from behind the circle. All players must kick the ball a minimum of two times. Any infractions result in a disqualification of the game, at which time a new game is initiated.

Fig. 3-8. Kick the ball and try to knock over the pins.

GAME 6

Major focus: Players kick and trap the ball while moving around in space. To free themselves to receive the ball, players must move to an open space.

Number of players: 6.

Equipment: A ball and a goal area.

Playing area: A rectangular area 30 × 60 feet (Fig. 3-9).

Rules: The objective is for the 3 offensive players to advance the ball down the field in an attempt to score a goal. Players must kick and trap the ball. Unless covered, 1 player may dribble the ball downfield and attempt to kick a goal. Two defensive players guard the offensive players while 1 defensive player guards the goal. When a defensive player comes to cover the dribbler, the ball should be passed to the open player. Kicks at the goal must be made from behind the 15-foot perimeter area. Any ball that goes out-of-bounds on the sidelines is given to the team that was last in possession. Teams take turns on offense and defense, each turn starting at one end line and finishing with a kick at the goal. Any interception or trap of a kick by a defensive player while the ball is in play ends the offensive set.

Scoring: One point is scored for each successful goal. One game is composed of 10 points.

Fouls and penalties: Being inside the perimeter area on a goal attempt is an infraction and results in a side out or the opposing team getting the ball. Holding, blocking, tripping, or preventing free movement of an offensive player is also an infraction and results in a free kick at the goal with only the goalkeeper guarding the area.

Fig. 3-9. Kick the ball to your teammates and try to score a goal.

CHAPTER FOUR

Striking with and without implements

Having discussed the process of kicking, which is a specialized form of striking with the foot, I will now present the remaining striking concepts. As a skill, striking involves the process of propelling objects through space by building up the momentum of the body prior to and without contact with the object. As stated in Chapter 1, after a maximum buildup of body momentum, the body makes only momentary contact with the object in a ballistic motion. Striking skills are a conglomeration of movements occurring in a variety of planes and under varying circumstances. One may strike balls at high, medium, and low levels in vertical, horizontal, and oblique planes with a heavy or light force. Several body parts may be used for purposes of striking. The arms, hands and/or fingers, feet, knee, and head are examples. Sometimes an implement is used as an extension of the arm to provide extra leverage, speed, and range of motion as the ball is struck. Examples of common striking implements are billiard cues, softball bats, golf clubs, tennis rackets, and badminton rackets.

PRINCIPLES OF HUMAN DEVELOPMENT

Earliest striking patterns seem to evolve from a swinging action of the arm. A young child can often swing an arm, a paddle, or a bat effectively before he is able to strike an object with some accuracy or for some distance. This is caused by visual perception development, as well as other principles of human development. The precision required to actually make contact with a stationary or moving object away from the body requires a mature form of eye-hand coordination. Farsightedness, tracking abilities, and figure-ground perception all pose problems for the young child. Large balls that provide a good color contrast with the background and have a controlled trajectory or rate of speed help during initial striking experiences. By the time a child is 11 or 12 years old, the eyes should be mature enough to perform more refined striking activities.

As indicated, other principles also affect the development of striking abilities. The large muscles of children develop before the small ones. Also, muscles develop from the center of the body to the periphery. Both concepts affect the ability of children to strike an object. As they gain experience and maturity, their striking actions are more controlled by their ability to execute fine muscle action at the periphery of the body. Whereas early attempts at striking are gross and in close to the body, more mature efforts are refined and are performed with good leverage away from the body.

The principle of unilateral-contralateral development is also noticeable in the maturation of the striking pattern. A child's initial striking attempts involve unilateral development. A right-handed child initially steps forward with the foot on the same side of the body as the striking action is made. As a result, there is no trunk rotation, which is also characteristic of an immature pattern. Gradually the child changes over to the more mature pattern of stepping forward with the opposite foot.

STRIKING

A discussion of the principles of human development leads to a consideration of the stages through which children pass on their way to mature striking patterns. As stated in the development of the unilateral-contralateral principle, the first, or *initial,* stage is characterized by an overarm pattern with little or no trunk rotation while the feet remain stationary or the foot on the same side of the striking arm moves forward. Whether the child is striking with or without an implement, these initial attempts are typified by a chopping action, or hitting down (top to bottom, high to low). Because of the chopping action, the child usually squarely faces the target to be struck, thus preventing any effective trunk rotation. According to research findings, most striking patterns, including serving a volleyball underhanded or striking with a bat or club, show that children from 2 to 6 years swing from the forearm in this anteroposterior plane. There is little buildup of body momentum, and a limited step forward shows a unilateral arm-leg pattern. (See initial stage in Fig. 4-1.)

If children are allowed to develop their striking patterns on their own without instruction, they seem to progress slowly from striking in a vertical plane downward to a more effective pattern in a predominantly horizontal

Fig. 4-1. Children learn striking patterns in stages.

plane. This second, or *elementary,* stage is characterized by abandoning the arm-dominated pattern to one in which there is a forward weight shift, a greater range of joint actions (whole arm), and some trunk rotation. This movement takes place in a sidearm pattern in which one or both arms are used and shows an initial blocking action of the leg after the step forward to allow for the forward weight shift and trunk rotation.

The third, or *mature,* stage of striking contains a basic sequence of three swiftly merging movements—step, turn, swing. During the step forward on the opposite foot the body weight is shifted in the direction of the intended hit, and the shoulders and arms are coiled in the opposite direction. To accomplish the turn, the hips and trunk are rotated in rapid succession in the same direction as the weight shift. To complete the action, the arms swing around and forward in close succession with the other rotary movements. Additional characteristics of the mature striking pattern involve a cocking of the arm, wrists, and/or implement during the backswing; more freedom in the swing with increased range of motion; a blocking action of the forward leg after the stride; and a more distinct uncocking of the effort action during the swing, emphasizing follow-through. In addition to the development of the sidearm pattern during the mature stage, children also become ready to perform the oblique pattern that is more characteristic of the golf swing. Even though this type of swing is usually allowed under conditions in which the player may take an unhurried preparatory swing at a stationary object, the oblique pattern appears to be the most complex to coordinate.

In an effort to overcome or counteract the tendency toward a slow maturation of striking patterns, it may be possible to structure situations in which children are encouraged and provided opportunities to practice those skills common to striking which are basically task oriented and sport skill related. The following situations are not favorable: older children and/or adults stand on home plate, face the pitcher and swing with immature form; flog at golf balls; demonstrate poor service, forehand, and backhand form in tennis; carry rather than strike volleyballs; and are one-hand dominant in handball. Instead, teachers should present controlled striking opportunities for children at an early age. Balls and striking implements should be developed that children can manage in terms of size, weight, and length. Balls should be suspended by a string from above or supported from below (batting tee) to ensure the development of proper timing and eye-hand coordination. Fear of the flight and speed of an approaching ball can be overcome with balloons and/or beach balls, which make the flight of the object slower, or the use of suspended balls or pitching machines, which control the flight of the object. Children also need opportunities to strike objects with forehand and backhand strokes, at high and low levels, and with varying amounts of force application in different directions. A variety of ball sizes and striking implements should also be used to ensure the development of mature patterns of striking.

STRIKING ACTIVITIES THROUGH EXPLORATION AND PROBLEM SOLVING

Individual

Without an implement

1. With just a little force, can you strike a ball up into the air and catch it before it touches the ground? Try to stay in your personal space. Practice with different body parts to perform this task—hands, arms, head, shoulder, knee, feet. Even try to use different surfaces of a single part—forehand, backhand, fist, and hand open.
2. As you gain more skill, begin using more force. How high can you strike the ball and still control it by catching it before it hits the ground?
3. Can you change levels as you strike and catch the ball? Strike the ball up into the air from low, medium, and high levels. Catch it at low, medium, and high levels. Strike the ball at a low level and catch it at a high level. Do the opposite.
4. Now try to strike the ball two or more times without catching it. As soon as you feel you are losing control, catch the ball and start again.
5. Begin moving around as you strike the ball into the air. First, strike the

Fig. 4-2. Strike the object with different body parts.

ball up and move to catch it before it bounces. Next, can you strike the ball so that you must move forward, backward, or sideward to catch it?

6. Remember to try activities 1 to 5 several times with different body parts and surfaces.
7. Are you able to change body parts while striking the ball? For purposes of control, if you need to allow the ball to bounce off the floor between strikes, do so.
8. See how long you are able to keep the ball in the air by striking it. Try not to strike the ball with the same body part two times in a row. Try not to use a bounce any more than you have to.
9. Perform activities 7 and 8 with different sizes, weights, and shapes.
10. Now change the direction in which you are striking the ball. Begin to strike it down toward the floor. Can you tap it with two hands and catch it? Can you tap it with one hand? If your feet get in the way because the ball bounces off them, kneel down with your feet behind you.
11. Try to bounce the ball continuously. Use both hands, one hand, the other hand, and alternate hands. What other body parts can you use to strike the ball toward the floor?
12. Without leaving your personal space, bounce the ball around your body. Can you do it clockwise? Can you bounce the ball through your legs?

13. Bounce the ball at high, medium, and low levels. Be aware of the change in speed of the bounce as you change levels.
14. Change the force of your dribble as you continue to work on the level of your dribble.
15. Begin moving around in space as you continue to dribble the ball. Can you move forward, backward, and sideward?
16. Vary your pathway on the floor as you strike the ball toward the floor and move in different directions.
17. Starting slowly, begin to increase your speed as you vary your pathway and direction while you strike the ball toward the floor.
18. Start, stop, and change directions and be as agile as possible as you continue to dribble the ball.
19. Vary the size and type of ball as you perform activities 10 to 18.
20. Now, again change the direction in which you are striking. Begin to strike the ball so that it goes away from your body. Can you hold the ball with one hand and strike it with the other? Alternate hands (reverse the process). Can you drop the ball and strike it while it is in the air or strike it on the rebound after the first bounce?
21. In what directions can you strike the ball away from your body?
22. At what levels can you strike the ball? Can you strike it at a low level with your fingers, hands, feet, etc. and make it travel away from you? What are the different ways you can strike the ball away from you at medium and high levels? Choose the ways that work best for you.
23. Can you throw the ball, balloon, or other object high into the air and strike it at such a high level that you actually jump and reach during your striking pattern?
24. Vary the force which you use to strike the ball. Sometimes use a little force for accuracy. Sometimes use great force for distance. Can you strike the ball for accuracy with great force?
25. Find a target (wastebasket, hoop, cardboard box, etc.) and try to strike the ball with just enough force so that it lands in the target. Vary your distance from the target as you strike the ball. Place the target flat on the floor, then suspend it in the air.
26. Suspend a ball from the ceiling. Stand near the target and begin striking the ball. Align your body in different ways: face the ball, then stand sideward. Can you strike the ball to and fro, side to side? Can you strike the ball when it is near your body? Far away? Can you hit the ball with your left hand, right hand, forehand, backhand, fist? With other body parts? Lie down and try to strike the ball as it swings above you. Strike the ball once and then stop it; do this several times. Then try to strike it repeatedly.
27. Find a wall and strike your ball against it. Can you strike the ball and

catch it before it bounces? Can you strike the ball against the wall and catch it after one bounce, two, etc.? Vary your distance from the wall—sometimes near, sometimes far.

28. Can you strike the ball continuously against a wall without allowing it to bounce, or with one bounce? Use your left hand, right hand, both hands. What is your body alignment as you strike the ball? Strike with a forehand and backhand motion.
29. Change the type of ball that you strike. Use balloons, tennis balls, beach balls, yarn balls, volleyballs, playground balls, etc. Perform each of the activities in nos. 20 to 28. What advantages do balloons and beach balls provide for striking activities? What are some unique ways you have discovered to use these pieces of equipment?

With an implement

1. Now perform striking activities with a racket, bat, stick, or club.* While working at a low level on the floor, strike a stationary object so that it goes away from you. Practice by varying the amount of force, distance, accuracy, and direction of the force application and then change hands. With the dominant hand strike the object forehanded and backhanded and in different directions. Change hands and repeat. Use oblique and horizontal swinging patterns. Strike the ball while you are stationary and on the move—sometimes slow and sometimes fast. Vary your pathway on the floor.
2. By suspending a ball from a string or supporting a ball from a batting tee, change the level of your swing to a medium range while striking the ball. Repeat the activities in no. 1 with a horizontal swinging pattern.
3. This time perform the same striking actions at a high level: throw the ball up into the air or have it suspended at a high level.
4. While continuing to vary the level of your striking action, use a wall against which the ball may rebound. As the ball rebounds off the wall, can you use your racket, or implement, to receive its force?† Can you strike the ball repeatedly as it rebounds off the wall? Change the striking pattern of your force application. With the dominant hand, strike forehanded and backhanded. Change hands and repeat. Vary your distance from the wall. Do not let the ball bounce. Let it bounce once, etc.
5. In nos. 2 to 4 you concentrated on striking the ball away from you at various levels. You varied your force application and direction of strike. You hit for distance and accuracy. Now try to go back and repeat activities 24 to 28

---

*Inexpensive nylon hose rackets, plastic hockey sticks, softball bats, *modified* paddle rackets, tennis rackets, badminton rackets, or golf clubs are recommended.

†Review the concepts of force absorption, or catching, in Chapter 2.

with your striking implements. Factors with which you should experiment are striking the ball continuously; aiming at a target; changing the size, weight, and texture of the balls and implements; and striking while stationary and on the move.

6. Next, use your implements to strike the ball or another object (badminton shuttlecock) in a vertical direction. Sometimes strike up, sometimes down. Perform activities 1 to 19 as you strike the ball by alternating your striking hands and varying the level at which you strike, the amount of force application, etc. Strike the ball with your implement while in a stationary position and on the move.
7. Make sure you change the implements with which you strike, as well as the objects you strike (balloon, yarn ball, tennis ball, table tennis ball, golf whiffle ball, softball, etc.).

Partner

Without an implement

1. Choose a partner and stand face to face about 10 feet apart. Try to strike a ball to your partner with just enough force so that he can catch it without moving out of his personal space. Try striking the ball while holding it with one hand, by dropping it and striking it before it hits the ground or after one bounce, or by throwing the ball up into the air and striking it.
2. As you work with your partner, begin to strike the ball continuously into the air while alternating turns. Are you able to use your hands to strike the ball? Can you use your left hand as well as your right? Remember that you must strike the ball underneath to send it up in the air to make it easier for your partner to return it to you.
3. Change levels as you strike the ball to your partner. Strike it at a low level and make it roll on the floor to your partner. Strike the ball to your partner at medium and high levels.
4. Change the direction of your striking actions and include each of the following: sometimes down at the floor, making the ball bounce before it reaches your partner; up in the air to your partner; and directly to your partner horizontally.
5. Can you make your partner move to the ball to strike it back? It is important to place the ball where it can be returned.
6. Begin to travel side by side down the field and strike the ball back and forth with your partner. Strike it in the air without allowing any bounces, or allowing one. Change your relationship with your partner as you two continue to strike the ball on the move.
7. Change the amount of force you use to try to strike the ball to your partner. Begin with a small amount while you are rather close to your partner. As you strike with more force, move farther away.

8. Work with your partner near a wall by alternating turns. Try to strike the ball after one bounce or no bounces. Try to put different types of spin on the ball as you strike it.
9. With your partner alternate dribbling and guarding. While one of you bounces or dribbles the ball continuously, the other attempts to guard and take the ball away. What should the dribbler do to prevent the ball from being stolen? (Never dribble the ball in front of the defender. Always keep your body between the ball and the defender.)
10. Vary the type and size of the ball you use when striking to your partner. Use balloons, volleyballs, marbles, tennis balls, yarn balls, playground balls, etc.

With an implement

1. Choose a partner and stand face to face about 10 to 12 feet apart. With your paddle or racket try to strike the ball to your partner with just enough force so that he can catch it without moving out of his personal space. The partner attempting to catch the ball may do so with the hands or the implement. It would be helpful to review the concepts of force absorption (catching) at this time.
2. While striking the ball directly to your partner with your paddle or racket, try striking it while holding it with one hand, by dropping the ball and striking it before it hits the ground or after one bounce, or by throwing the ball up into the air and striking it.
3. Attempt to strike the ball continuously with your partner. Try striking the ball while volleying in the air or after one bounce. How many times can you strike it repeatedly under control? If the ball gets out of control, stop it and start again.
4. Are you able to strike the ball with your paddle or racket equally well with each hand? Can you strike the ball forehanded and backhanded? Can you control the paddle or racket best with one or both hands? Can you strike the ball better when it is close to your body or when you have to extend or reach a little for it?
5. Change levels as you strike the ball. Strike it sometimes at high, medium, and low levels.
6. Strike the ball with your paddle or racket in a variety of ways and from a variety of positions. Are you able to return the ball to your partner from either side of your body?
7. As you stand still, strike the ball to make your partner move to receive it. Make the receiver move up, back, right, and left to receive the ball.
8. Can you strike the ball while on the move? To return the ball to your partner, use your paddle or racket to strike it as you move forward, backward, and to the side.

Fig. 4-3. Bat the ball as far as you can.

9. Change your relationship with your partner as you continue to strike the object with your implement. Move from near to far. Move side to side. Strike a lead pass to your partner.
10. Apply varying amounts of force with your striking implement as you attempt to strike for distance and/or accuracy. (See Fig. 4-3.)
    a. Can you bat a ball far? Can you bunt it?
    b. Can you drive a golf ball far? Can you use the irons? Can you putt at a target?
    c. Can you strike a badminton shuttlecock deep into the backcourt? Can you drop the shuttlecock just over the net?
    d. Can you drive a field hockey ball or ice hockey puck at a goal from varying distances? Can you use a little force to control the ball or puck as you dribble it downfield?
    e. Can you apply a large amount of force with a billiard ball to break a group of balls or a small amount of force to finesse a soft corner shot?
    f. Think of other sports in which variations of force application with an implement are important. (Tennis, racquetball, squash, polo, etc.)
11. Can you control your striking action with the implement to determine whether the ball will travel on the ground or in the air? Where do you contact the ball to make it travel on the ground? Travel in the air?
12. Vary the implements with which you strike and the objects that you strike as you continue to strike with a partner. Use nylon rackets, tennis rackets, golf clubs, hockey sticks, badminton rackets, softball bats, etc., along with appropriate types of objects. Experiment by striking in different ways, directions, and levels and with different amounts of force.

13. Cooperate with a partner as you two use your implements to move an object across the floor or field to score a goal. Take turns aiming at the target. Vary the target size.
14. Play against your partner as you use your implement to strike your object toward the target or goal. One partner acts as the goalie while the other attempts to strike the object into the target.

GUIDED DISCOVERY PROBLEMS FOR STRIKING

Without an implement

1. A striking action allows you to build up your body momentum prior to applying force to an object. What body parts can you use effectively to strike an object? (Fingers, hands [different parts of the hand], shoulder, elbow, head, knee, and foot.)
2. With only your hands to strike the ball, how many different ways can you apply force? (Children should discover that the same weight transfer concepts for locomotion apply in this situation.) The ball may be struck by one hand repeatedly, one to the other (one to one), one to two, two to one, two to two.
3. In what directions can you impart force as you strike an object? (Forward, backward, sideward, up, and down.)
4. In what type of pathways do objects travel after being struck by your body? (Linear—straight forward, backward, up, and down and curvilinear—with an arc.)
5. If it is your intention to strike an object vertically into the air, how can your body best apply force to accomplish this task? How can you make a ball travel straight up so that it comes back down to you without your having to travel to receive it? (Bend at the ankle, knee, hip, and arm joints to get under the ball. Apply force directly under the ball to send it up. When striking the ball at a high level, the fingers are pointed up and the thumbs toward the midline of the body. When striking at a low level the fingers are pointed down and the thumbs pointed away from the body.)
6. If it is your intention to strike an object directly down at the floor, how can your body apply force to accomplish this task? How can you bounce, tap, or dribble a ball so that it bounces right back up to you? (Apply force directly over the ball to send it down. Apply the correct amount of force to be able to control the ball. If you apply too much force, the ball will bounce over your head, and then you will not be able to continue bouncing it. If you apply too little force, the ball will stop bouncing. To control the ball, your body must stay close to it, and it should be bounced at a medium level.)
7. If it is your intention to send an object away from you in a forward, backward, or sideward direction with a linear or curvilinear pathway, how

can your body best apply force to accomplish this task? (Apply force in the direction of the intended motion. If you want the ball to go forward, you must strike behind the ball. This pattern is used most often in sports and is called a "horizontal swing." If you want the ball to travel in an arc, you must strike the ball in an oblique fashion somewhat to the side and under simultaneously.)

8. As you execute the striking pattern, what can you do with your body to contact the ball efficiently?
   a. Shift body weight in the direction of the intended hit.
   b. Position the body so that the hips and trunk can be rotated in rapid succession in the direction of the weight shift for sidearm and oblique patterns.
   c. Extend the part of the body that strikes the object to gain maximum leverage and range of motion.
   d. Windup or cock the joints in action during the preparatory phase of motion.
   e. Keep your eyes on the object (watch the object).
   f. Follow through.
   g. Move toward the ball so as to meet it. Do not wait for the ball to come to you.
9. At the time of contact, how should the force be applied to achieve maximum control of the object? (Contact the ball with as big or wide and level surface area as possible. This means fingertip control in dribbling a basketball and a two-hand, or forearm, set in volleyball, for example.)
10. If you want to strike a ball for distance, how could you accomplish this task? (Apply a large amount of force.) Which body parts work better than others when trying to strike for distance? (The arms work best.) Why? (Leverage and range of motion.) At what angle should you strike a ball to gain the greatest distance? (45 degrees.)
11. If you want to strike a ball repeatedly for control and accuracy, how could you accomplish this task? (Apply a little force. Keep the ball relatively close to the body. Apply the force in a straight up or down direction.)
12. Set up targets or have a partner stand at three different distances (10, 20, and 30 feet). Try to strike the ball so that it travels straight to the target. As the distance increases, how much force do you have to apply to get the ball to travel farther? How does the angle of the flight of the ball change as your distance from the target increases?
13. Set up targets or have a partner stand at three different distances (5, 10, and 20 feet). Use balls of three different weights and sizes (beach ball, volleyball, and tennis ball) to strike at the targets. How much force does it take to propel balls of different weights and sizes? (It takes more force to strike heavier balls greater distances. Because of air resistance, it also

may require more force to propel a large ball with a small mass a great distance.)

14. Stand 10 feet from a wall and strike the ball against the wall. Can you catch it before it bounces? Can you catch it after only one bounce? As you strike the ball against the wall, try to apply different types of spin on the ball. Can you put topspin or backspin on the ball? Can you make the ball spin to the left and right? What happens to the ball when it strikes the wall as it is spinning in one of these directions? How would this affect your play in a game situation?
15. Try to strike a ball or object so that it rolls or slides a specific distance along the ground (5, 10, and 20 feet). Use balls of different sizes and weights (marbles, golf balls, tennis balls, hockey pucks, volleyballs). How much force should you apply to get the object to travel along the floor that specific distance? Which body parts should you use to strike the objects? How does the force of your strike vary as you change the objects you strike along the floor? (The heavier the object, the more force must be applied.) What role does friction play in the distance an object moves along the floor? Once momentum is built up, which object takes longer or more force to stop—a heavy object or a light one?
16. Repeat experiments 12 to 15 while trying to strike objects through the air at targets placed at varying distances and/or various levels.
17. Practice striking at balls or other objects that are in a stationary position as well as moving. What can your body do to prepare to strike a moving object?
18. In a net-oriented game, under what conditions do you try to strike the ball deep into your opponents' court? When do you attempt to spike the ball? When do you drop the ball just over the net? Where do you try to serve the ball—forecourt or backcourt? Why?
19. In field-oriented games, under which conditions do you attempt a drive or smash with great force? When do you try passing shots? Shots with spin on the ball? Drop shots? Why?
20. In field-oriented games in which dribbling or bouncing occurs, how can you best protect the ball from an opponent while dribbling on the run or changing directions? (Always try to keep your body between your opponent and the ball. If you must change directions by bouncing the ball in front of your opponent, lower your dribble and increase its rate [dribble faster].)

With an implement

1. What kinds of implements are used in sports to strike objects? (Golf clubs, billiard cues, badminton rackets, tennis rackets, softball and hardball bats, hockey sticks, etc.) Why are they used? (To help the body apply force to objects.) What advantage do they serve? (They allow a greater range of

motion to be achieved, more force to be applied, and more leverage and better mechanical advantage. As a result, an object has the potential to travel farther at faster rates of speed.) While gaining all these benefits, what is sacrificed? (The body has to expend great amounts of energy to manipulate the objects, and accuracy may be lost.) If the body has to use a large amount of energy to manipulate sport implements, what can be done to help young children whose muscles are not mature? (Implements can be modified with shorter handles, lighter weights, or smaller sizes. In addition, the object to be struck can be controlled through suspension or support.)

2. Practice striking a ball or another object with your body only. Which body parts did you choose? How much force did you use? How far did the object travel? Now use a nylon hose racket, bat, modified tennis racket, hockey stick, etc. to strike the object. How much force did you use? How far did the object travel? Compare force application and distance traveled with and without the use of implements.
3. Try to strike for accuracy a ball or another object toward a target such as a cardboard box, bowling pin, line on the floor, or hoops suspended in the air. How and where do you apply the force? (When attempting to strike for accuracy, a controlled force must be applied directly behind, over, or under the direction of the intended motion.)
4. In addition to applying a maximum amount of force to an object, there are times in games when you wish to strike an object with only a small amount of force—putting in golf, drop shot in tennis, bunt in baseball, etc. How is this accomplished? (In an effort to develop a gentle touch, try to be sensitive to how the implement is held—firm, yet loose. In activities in which the ball or object is traveling toward the player, try to give with, absorb, or receive part of the force of the object as it is struck in the opposite direction.)
5. What are some different types of ways in which an object may be struck with an implement? (Vertical, horizontal, or oblique swing or punching actions may be used.) Under which conditions are each used?
6. In addition to the different planes through which one strikes, sometimes a racket or club is used on different or alternating sides of the body. What are the differences between a left-handed or right-handed swing in golf or baseball? What are the similarities? What are the differences in a forehand or backhand strike in tennis, table tennis, paddleball, etc.? What are the similarities?
7. At what levels can you strike an object with your implement? What types of strokes work best at each level? (At a low level the oblique stroke works best. At a medium level, sidearm, but sometimes a punching action is used, as in billiards. At a high level the vertical stroke works best.)
8. Practice striking an object with your implement for purposes of getting

Fig. 4-4. Strike the object along the ground.

the object to fly through the air. Can you strike the object into the air from the ground or higher into the air from a low or medium level? Where must you contact the object to make it travel in the air?

9. As you strike an object with your implement, can you make it travel along the ground? Where must you contact the object to get it to travel on the ground? (See Fig. 4-4.)
10. Practice applying different types of spin on the ball as you strike it with your implement. How can you put topspin or backspin on the ball? Can you make it spin to the left or right? How does a spinning ball react as it bounces on the floor? How could this be used to your advantage in sports?
11. In a net-oriented game your opponent is crowding the front line, or net. What are some ways to strategically counteract this behavior? (You could attempt a lob shot over your opponent's head to the backcourt or hit a shot down the sideline or alley.)
12. What kinds of shots would strategically best be used against an opponent who played the backcourt mostly? (The best shot choices would be a drop shot just over the net, one with topspin that would keep the ball low and bounce twice in rapid succession, or one with backspin that would bounce and make the opponent charge for the ball.)
13. In a field-oriented game, under what conditions do you try to strike an object for distance? Try to hit the ball into the air? Try to apply only a little force to the ball? Use golf, baseball, and other sports for your examples.

COOPERATIVE AND COMPETITIVE GAMES

The remainder of this chapter is intended to combine the qualities of movement with various striking concepts in an effort to create major focuses, or themes, that stimulate games between and among children. It is your role as the teacher to help children learn about and play within the framework, or guidelines, as outlined in Chapter 1. After the children have become familiar with various playing areas, field designs, open and closed games, time factors, scoring systems, strategies, penalties for rule infractions, etc., they may design their own games according to their own level of abilities and interests. Initial games will tend to be cooperative in nature with a few simple rules. Later the games will involve more rules, a higher level of strategy, and competition.

■ Given a ball (beachball, volleyball, playground ball, basketball, etc.) or another object such as a balloon, make up a game with your partners (group of 2 to 6 players). Use one or more of the following rules as the focus, or theme, of your game.

Rules

1. Strike the ball up at a high level. Allow one or more bounces on the floor.
2. Strike the ball out at a medium or low level. Use a wall (to allow for rebounds), a net, or a field design.
3. Strike the ball down at the floor.
4. Stress relationships in your game. Can you be face to face, side by side, near or far from your teammates or opponents?
5. Use a target to determine how accurately you can strike the ball. Vary your distance from the target.
6. Vary the force with which you strike the ball.
7. Make up a game to determine how high or far you can strike the ball.
8. Strike the ball while all players remain in a stationary position.
9. Strike the ball while all players are moving.

■ Given a ball or another object and a striking implement such as a bat, racket, club, mallet, or cue, make up a game with your partners. Use one or more of the following rules as the focus of your game.

Rules

1. Strike the object with your implement so that it rolls or slides along the floor, ground, or table surface.
2. Strike the object away from your body at a medium level with your implement. Allow one or no bounces.
3. Strike the object with your implement in a vertical pathway. Stress striking the object into a high level.
4. Stress accuracy as you strike your object at a target.

5. Focus on range as you work with a partner, sometimes striking while near your teammate, sometimes while farther away.
6. Concentrate on relationships as you strike the object with your implement while on the move. Strike the object while face to face or side by side a teammate or opponent.
7. Vary the amount of force you use to strike the object with your implement.
8. Attempt to strike an object to a teammate while being guarded by an opponent.

■ Given an object, a striking implement, and a hoop, bowling pin, tire, scoop, plastic bottle or another piece of equipment, make up a game with your friends. Use one or more of the following rules as the focus of your game.

Rules

1. Place a hoop, tire, or cardboard box horizontally or down on the floor and use your implement to strike your object (ball, shuttlecock) into the target. Vary your distance from the target and the resulting force application accordingly.
2. Suspend or hold a tire or hoop in a vertical plane and use your implement to strike your object through the target. Start with the target in a stationary position; then roll or swing the tire or hoop to provide a moving target. Vary your distance from the target.
3. Use bowling pins, plastic bottles, or high jump standards as targets or goals as you aim to hit one of the targets. Strike the ball or object at a low level to roll or slide at or between the goal. Strike the object at medium or high levels to go through or over the goal. Vary your distance from the target. Change your style of strokes and the amount of force application.
4. Attempt to strike your object at or through a goal or target while someone is guarding you or the goal.
5. Strike objects into the air at various levels with your implement and use a plastic scoop to catch the object before it touches the ground or after one bounce.

SAMPLE GAMES

GAME 1

Major focus: Strike a marble* for accuracy with the fingers; "shoot" it into a target from various distances.

Number of players: 2 to 4.

Equipment: Marbles and any kind of a box.

Playing area: A flat surface (Fig. 4-5).

Rules: The objective of the game is to shoot the marbles at the target and obtain as high a score as possible. Players take ten attempts from each distance and count their cumulative score.

Scoring: Points are counted according to the hole in which the marble enters—10, 5, or 3.

Fouls and penalties: Any marble struck from in front of a line does not count in the score, and the player loses this turn.

---

*For a variety of marble games the reader is referred to the Ferritti marble book (1975).

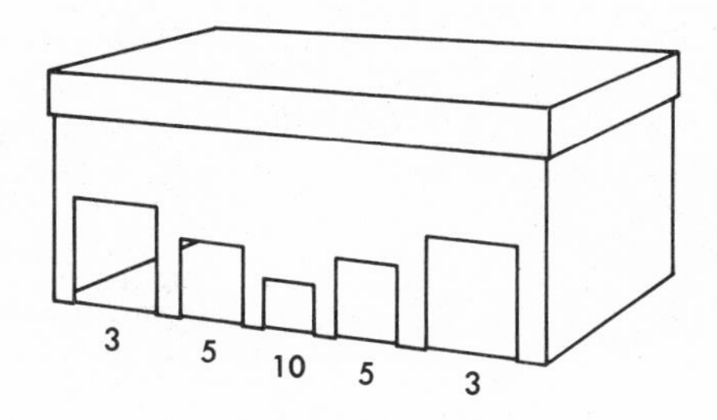

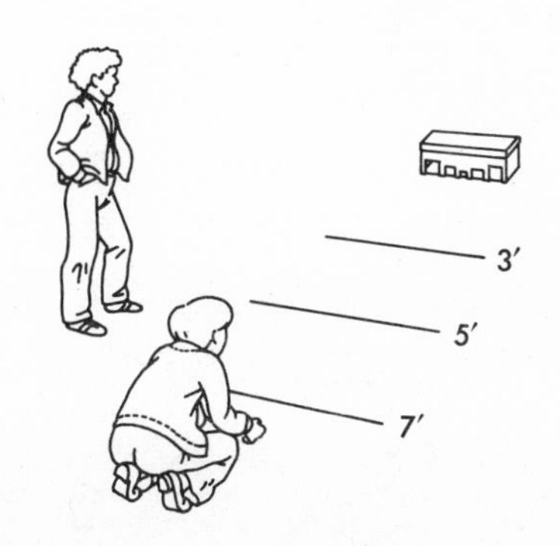

Fig. 4-5. Strike the marble through one of the holes.

GAME 2

Major focus: Strike the ball alternately while playing with a partner in a wall or net game.

Number of players: 2 to 4.

Equipment: A nylon hose racket, paddle racket, or tennis racket and appropriate ball.

Playing area: A rectangular playing area with a wall at one end or a net in the middle. The game may be played with or without an implement, as in racquetball or handball. (See Fig. 4-6.)

Rules: The server may toss the ball in the air or allow it to bounce once before striking it. The ball must travel over the net and land in the service area or strike the wall above the line and land in the service area. After the service, players must alternate striking the ball. The ball may bounce only once before it must be returned. A ball will be played continuously until it strikes the ground twice or goes out-of-bounds. Only the server may score points. If the server strikes the ball out-of-bounds or allows the ball to bounce on the ground twice while it is being volleyed, he loses the serve. If the receiver of the serve strikes the ball out-of-bounds or allows the ball to bounce on the ground twice while it is being volleyed, he loses a point.

Scoring: Each point counts 2. A game is played to 20 points. One set is the winner of 3 games.

Fouls and penalties: Each server has two attempts to strike the ball into the service area. If he misses on the first try, a second try is awarded. Two misses causes a loss of serve.

Variation: This game may be played on a modified court without rackets by striking the ball with the hands.

Fig. 4-6. Take turns striking the ball against a wall.

GAME 3

Major focus: Strike the ball down toward the ground or off a wall into specific target areas.

Number of players: 2 to 5.

Equipment: A ball such as a tennis ball or playground ball.

Playing area: A sidewalk area near a wall or building (Fig. 4-7).

Rules: The purpose of this experience is to adapt commonly known sidewalk* games to emphasize the concept of learning to strike a ball in a downward direction without an implement. In the two- and four-square games, players straddle their sidewalk squares. The server in box A strikes the ball into box B. Then, after the ball bounces, player B is free to strike the ball into any box he chooses (in two-square, to box A). The one who makes an error receives 1 point. After a point all players move one box clockwise, and the player now in box A becomes the server. As in all boxball games, putting spin on the ball is important.

In the Chinese handball game, player A serves the ball to player B. The ball must hit the ground, then the wall. In the same manner, B strikes the ball to C, C to D, D to E, E back to D, etc. Any player who misses or errs in any way receives 1 point and is moved to square E.

Scoring: Players accumulate 1 point at a time until they total 10, at which time the game is terminated and a new one started. Lowest score wins.

---

*Readers who are interested in enhancing their knowledge of other street games such as stickball and batting games (Game 8) and their variations are referred to the Ferritti game book (1975).

Fig. 4-7. Strike the ball toward the ground or off a wall.

GAME 4

Major focus: Use a racket to strike the ball, shuttlecock, or other object continuously with a partner without allowing the object to touch the ground.

Number of players: 2 to 4.

Equipment: Nylon hose rackets, table tennis rackets, paddle rackets, or badminton rackets; a light ball, balloon, or shuttlecock; and a net or a rope.

Playing area: A rectangular area approximately 20 × 40 feet (Fig. 4-8).

Rules: This is a cooperative game in which players work together to see how many consecutive times they can strike the object over the net without allowing it to touch the ground or go out-of-bounds. As players gain more skill, they can concentrate on specific shots such as forehand, backhand, lob, and drive.

Scoring: One point is counted (by a player or a doubles team) for each consecutive hit. Players compete against themselves to see how high they can get their score.

Fouls and penalties: When a ball or object touches the ground or goes out-of-bounds, this constitutes a dead ball, and play must again be started at zero.

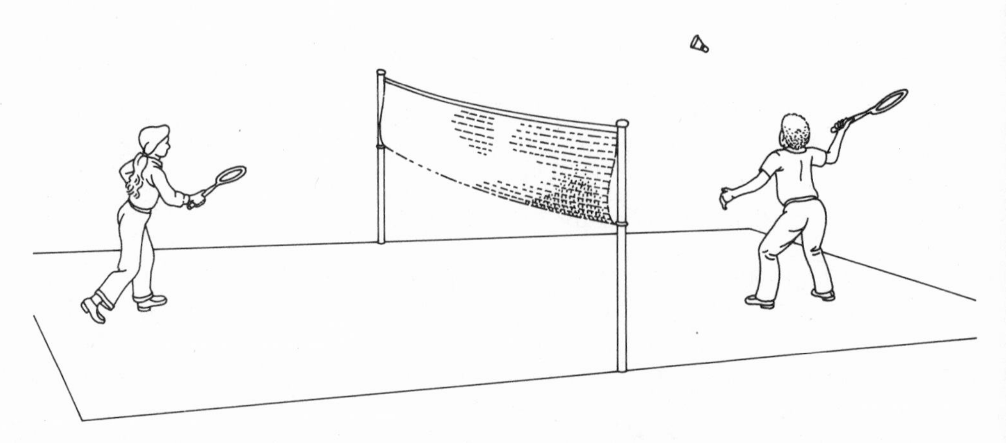

Fig. 4-8. Strike the object over the net.

GAME 5

Major focus: With a racket, strike the ball, shuttlecock, or other object over the net and into your opponent's court.

Number of players: 2 to 4.

Equipment: Two rackets, a birdie or ball, and a bench, rope, or net to serve as a dividing line.

Playing area: A rectangular playing area 20 × 40 feet (Fig. 4-8).

Rules: A coin is tossed, and the winner chooses to serve first or defend a specific court side. The server stands at the back right side of the court and serves either underhanded or overhanded. Three chances are allowed for a successful serve. Players volley the ball back and forth over the net until the object touches the floor or goes out-of-bounds. An object touching a boundary line is considered inbounds.

Scoring: A point is scored by a player or a doubles team any time the opponent does not return the object over the net or when the opponent strikes the object out-of-bounds. When a team scores 20 points, it is declared the winner.

GAME 6

Major focus: Dribble the ball repeatedly in an attempt to advance the ball downcourt. Guard an opponent in an attempt to stop an advance or to take the ball away.

Number of players: 2.

Equipment: A basketball or playground ball.

Playing area: A rectangular area approximately 15 × 60 feet (Fig. 4-9).

Rules: Players take turns on offense and defense. The objective for the offensive player is to dribble the ball downcourt to the opposite end. The offensive player should use proper dribbling skills such as dribbling with either hand, keeping the ball low, and keeping the body between the ball and the opponent. The objective for the defensive player is to stop the offensive player from dribbling downcourt or to take the ball away. The defensive player should learn to use the boundary lines to advantage, to get a good position (no reaching in), and to steal the ball when circumstances permit.

Scoring: Scores may be kept on the basis of the time it takes for the player to get from one end to the other or the number of feet the dribbler is able to advance the ball.

Fouls and penalties: Dribbling the ball out-of-bounds stops the clock or results in a loss of turn. Fouling a person while dribbling by slapping, reaching in, or making contact stops the action and allows the dribbler to regain control. Penalty points may also be subtracted from the defensive player in terms of points or added time. The severity of the penalty should be determined by the players.

Fig. 4-9. Dribble the ball past your partner.

GAME 7

Major focus: Strike the ball at a low level with an implement in an attempt to hit a target.

Number of players: 1 to 6.

Equipment: A croquet set or broomsticks, mallets, or field hockey sticks; balls; and clothing hangers for targets.

Playing area: An open space at least 20 × 60 feet (Fig. 4-10).

Rules: The rules of croquet apply in this situation. Players get one turn to strike the ball. If on their turn they roll the ball through one or more of the wickets, or targets, they get one extra turn to strike the ball for each wicket passed through. On the first turn a player usually knocks the ball through the two nearest wickets and therefore earns two more turns. Play is conducted in a weaving manner from the inside wicket to the outside, etc. until each has been passed through and players return to the starting position. After the first turn, players get only one opportunity to strike the ball unless that turn causes their ball to go through a wicket, at which time they earn a bonus shot.

Scoring: The game may be scored by the least number of shots to complete the course.

Variations: Players may make a rule that if a player can hit another's ball, both may place their two balls together, place their foot on their ball, and use the mallet to strike their opponent's ball off course. A rule may also be made that any player completing the course becomes "wild." The "wild" player may then try to strike his ball in an attempt to contact another's ball, at which time they are eliminated from the game.

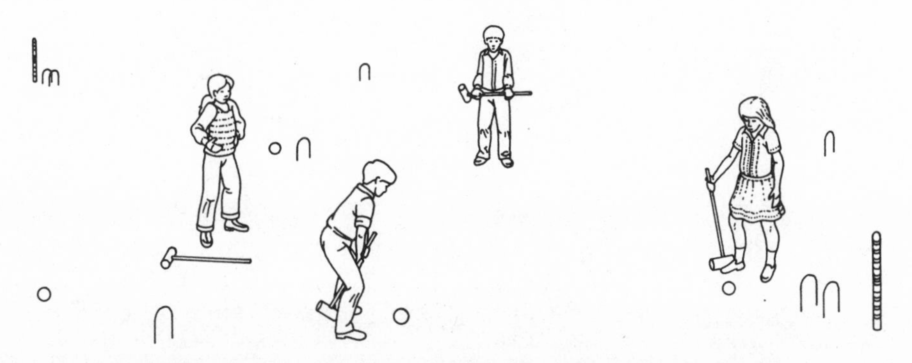

Fig. 4-10. Use your club to strike the ball through the target.

GAME 8

Major focus: Throw the ball up in the air and bat (strike) it as far as possible.
Number of players: 3.
Equipment: A softball and bat, or broomstick and tennis ball.
Playing area: A street or open field area (Fig. 4-11).
Rules: The batter throws the ball up and hits it and is allowed two servings. A hit past the short fielder is a single; past the first chalked line, a double; past some landmark or another line, a triple; and past the outfielder, a homer. A ball caught on the ground or in the air by the short fielder or in the air by the outfielder is an out. Two outs are permitted per inning. When the batter makes two outs, the short fielder becomes the batter, the outfielder moves to the short field, and the batter becomes the outfielder.
Scoring: One point per run is allowed. Five innings constitute a game.

Fig. 4-11. Bat the ball into the outfield.

GAME 9

Major focus: Strike the ball up into the air and over the net. Cooperatively work with teammates to bump and/or set the ball so that another player may strike it over the net.

Number of players: 10 to 12.

Equipment: A volleyball, volleyball standards, and a net.

Playing area: A volleyball court 30 × 60 feet (Fig. 4-12).

Rules: The server must serve the ball over the net. Players on the receiving side must return the ball with an appropriate striking action either themselves or by setting the ball to another player. Whoever strikes the ball over the net scoots under the net and begins to play on the opposite side. The objective of the game is to cooperate with each member on both teams to successfully get all members of the team to change sides. All team members must cooperate to help everyone exchange sides. The only time an exchange of sides does not take place is when the ball touches the floor, goes out-of-bounds, or is served.

Scoring: There is no scoring. A game is successfully completed when every member exchanges sides. A group may compete with themselves for their fastest time or fewest number of strikes.

Fig. 4-12. Strike the ball over the net and then change sides.

GAME 10

Major focus: Strike the ball at a low level with an implement while moving around in space. To free yourself to receive the ball or puck, you must move to an open space.

Number of players: 6 to 9.

Equipment: Floor hockey sticks, brooms, a plastic puck, a ball, and a goal area.

Playing area: A rectangular area 30 × 60 feet (Fig. 4-13).

Rules: The objective of the game is for the 3 offensive players to advance the ball or puck downfield in an attempt to score a goal. Players must strike the ball or puck with their stick and make it roll or slide along the floor. Unless covered, one player may dribble the object down the field with the stick and attempt to strike it into the goal. When a defensive player covers the dribbler, the object should be passed to an open player. Two defensive players guard the offensive players while 1 defensive player guards the goal. Attempts at scoring a goal must be struck from behind the 15-foot perimeter line. When the ball or puck goes out-of-bounds on the sidelines, it goes to the team that was last in possession. Teams take turns on offense and defense, each turn beginning at one end line and ending with an attempt at the goal. Any interception or steal of the ball or puck by a defensive player while the ball is in play ends the offensive set.

Scoring: Three points are scored for each successful goal. One game is composed of 15 points.

Fouls and penalties: The following infraction results in a side out or the opposing team getting the ball or puck:

1. Being inside the perimeter area on a goal attempt.

The following infractions result in a free attempt at the goal with only the goalkeeper guarding the area:

1. Raising one's stick above hip level.
2. Holding, tripping, or preventing an offensive player from free movement.

Fig. 4-13. Strike the object to an open teammate who will attempt a goal.

GAME 11

Major focus: Cooperate with teammates to successfully strike the ball over a net or barrier.

Number of players: 6.

Equipment: One ball and a net or imaginary boundary.

Playing area: A rectangular area about 10 × 20 feet (Fig. 4-14).

Rules: The game is essentially a modified volleyball game. The objective is for all 3 players on one side to successfully strike the ball into the air before sending it over the net, or boundary. The ball may not touch the ground unless all players agree to modify the game to allow one bounce between striking the ball each time.

Scoring: Unlike most games that allow scoring when the other team makes a mistake, the only way to score a point in this game is when teammates cooperate successfully. One point is scored each time all 3 players of a team strike the ball before sending it over to the other team. A game consists of 10 points.

Fig. 4-14. Help your teammates strike the ball over the net.

CHAPTER FIVE

Additional game-playing concepts

The three previous chapters of this text concentrated on the manipulation concepts of throwing, catching, kicking, trapping, and a variety of striking patterns because they are of primary importance in game implementation. This chapter will have two primary focuses. The first is to consider other manipulative and locomotor concepts that are also important to the development of game-playing skills. The second focus is to stress the importance of combining manipulative concepts when playing games. Except for games played by children during their period of egocentricity and specific exploration and games of the closed type, most games actually involve combinations of manipulative skills. Indeed, most open games that lead toward the conventional games of adults include several manipulative concepts. For example, basketball and its lead-up games involve throwing, catching, striking and carrying, along with running and jumping. Football-type games include throwing, catching, kicking, and carrying, along with a variety of running and blocking skills. As in previous chapters, each of the manipulative and locomotor concepts will be discussed prior to the statement of exploration and problem solving and guided discovery that lead to the development of each of the concepts. The chapter will be completed by cooperative and competitive game situations with some sample games.

CARRYING

As a manipulative concept, carrying is often overlooked. There is little if any research evidence available that concentrates on the development of carrying as a skill. Carrying is evidenced as an early maturational pattern in infants in the prehensive actions of reaching and grasping. The objective of carrying is to maintain contact with the ball. Because the muscles of flexion develop before those of extension, that it is somewhat natural for children to hold on to objects is a reasonable assumption. And yet at stages of their development, children are often clumsy or fumble fingered.

The refined skills of carrying that need to be developed by elementary school children involve carrying an object in one or both hands while on the move. In some games it is important to hold the ball in close to the body with both hands to protect it from players who might try to take it away. In other games a player may carry the ball in one hand or arm, usually the one away from the defensive player, so that the body may be used to protect the ball. At a time when a player is moving, it also becomes important to be able to transfer the ball from one hand to the other without fumbling. As a way to maintain continuous contact with the ball, children should also learn how to hand it to another person while standing still, moving in the same direction, or moving in opposite directions. In some games it is also important to learn to carry an object with the use of an implement. Carrying an object with or without an implement should be varied in many ways to make the skill as versatile as possible. Children should learn to carry and hand off the ball at different levels while moving at different speeds and in different directions and pathways. The size, weight, and shape of the ball, along with the type of carrying implement, should also be varied.

LOCOMOTOR CONCEPTS

In addition to manipulative concepts, most games invariably involve some form of locomotion. *Locomotion* may be defined as movement of the body through space. For purposes of game implementation this discussion of locomotor forms will be limited to those which are used most often in games—walk, run, leap, jump, hop, slide, gallop, and skip.

Walking, running, and leaping may be defined as the transfer of weight from one foot to the other. In *walking* at least one foot is always in contact with the ground. In *running* there is a momentary flight phase, as well as an increased stride and pace. In *leaping* the flight phase is emphasized as the performer tries to gain height and remain in the air as long as possible. These patterns all involve arm and leg opposition. The development of walking and running may be categorized into three stages, just as the manipulative patterns can. During the first, or *initial,* stage the legs are held rather stiff and the base of support is rather wide. Because of a lack of flexion, the toddler tends to rotate the toes and knees in an outward direction. The arms swing only in a short arc with little flexion at the elbow. To counterbalance the leg action, the arms may hook across the front of the trunk toward the midline. During the second, or *elementary,* stage the child's stride increases, and the base of support narrows. There is a more complete leg action, as evidenced by more knee flexion during recovery and greater leg extension during takeoff. The arms also swing through a greater arc, with a forward-backward action rather than across the front of the body. Once a child reaches the third, or *mature,* stage of walking or running, the arm and leg action becomes most efficient. During the recovery phase of the leg action the knee is raised high (for running). The support leg is bent slightly at contact and extends completely at takeoff. The arms swing through the vertical plane in opposition to the legs and are flexed at varying degrees, depending on the speed of the gait. The arms or legs have little rotary action at this point. The amount of bobbing, or up-and-down action, of the body decreases during each stage. Little research has been conducted on the developmental stages of the leap. However, because of the difficulty of mastering the extended flight phase and the balance required in landing, it is thought that children should practice this skill after gaining some mastery of walking and running.

In an attempt to develop walking, running, and leaping patterns that are adaptable in many types of game situations, children should participate in a variety of experiences. They should start slowly and increase their speed while moving forward, backward, and sideward. They should learn how to start, stop, and change directions quickly and efficiently. Moving forcefully as well as lightly while changing the pathway—direct, curved, and zigzag—is important to a child's walking, running, and leaping patterns. Running, walking, and climbing up and down various gradients and textures—along with moving over, under, around, between, and through various obstacles—should also be incorporated into their experiences. Children love to practice these skills while chasing and fleeing others or while combining these skills with the manipulative concepts already described.

Of the remaining locomotor concepts, jumping has perhaps been researched most. *Jumping* may be defined as a one- or two-foot takeoff and a two-foot landing with balance. One may attempt to jump for distance (long jump) or for height (vertical jump). At the *initial* stage the jump of a preschool child may be nothing more than a stepping action because children have difficulty coordinating both sides of the body at the same time. When jumping from a height, the child may actually step down. As a result, the jump has almost no flight phase. Lack of an efficient flight phase at the initial stage of the jump is further caused by a limited preparatory crouch; incomplete extension of the legs at the hips, knees and ankles; and lack of coordination of the arms, as well as ineffective arm use, to aid the jump. During the second, or *elementary,* stage the arms are employed more effectively during the preparatory action of the jump. They initiate forward momentum of the body at takeoff and then are held at the side for balance during landing. The action of

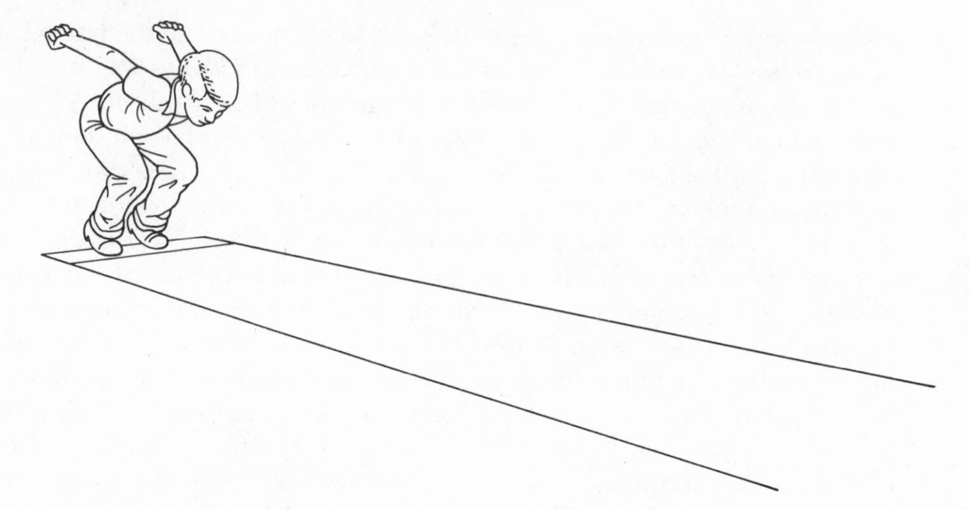

Fig. 5-1. Children learn to jump in stages.

the legs is also more efficient, since the legs extend more at the hips, knees, and ankles at takeoff. At this stage a child is practicing both one- and two-foot takeoffs from a stationary position and while on the move. The *mature* jumping action during the third stage is also characterized by efficient coordination of the arms, trunk, and legs. The arms move upward in a swinging action and are held high, initiating the upward body action. In coordination the trunk, hips, knees, and ankles make a full extension to complete the jumping action. When long jumping, the trunk at takeoff is extended at about a 45-degree angle. When landing from a jump, the legs bend at the ankles, knees, and hips to absorb the body's force efficiently. (See Fig. 5-1.)

To ensure that children develop a mature jumping pattern which may be implemented in a variety of game situations, children should participate in a variety of experiences. They should be encouraged to jump with one- and two-foot takeoffs in forward, backward, and sideward directions. Their jumping actions should include a large amount and a small amount of force as they attempt to jump once for height or distance or rhythmically several times in succession. Children should be encouraged to jump from various reasonable heights, beginning at a low level. They should also practice jumping in and out of various obstacles; jumping while catching, throwing, or striking various objects; and combining various other locomotor and/or manipulative actions with jumping.

At times hopping, sliding, galloping, and skipping are important locomotor concepts that are included in children's games. A *hop* is the transfer of weight from one foot to the same foot after a brief flight phase. A *slide* is a sideward movement of the body initiated by a combination of two simple locomotor movements—a leap-step. One foot always leads—the left when moving left, the right when moving right. After an initial emphasized leaping step in the direction of movement, the trail leg slides sideways close to the lead leg and receives the body weight, at which time another sliding step may begin. A *gallop,* like the slide, is a leap-step. The only difference is in the direction of movement, which is forward or backward. One foot, left or right, always leads, and the other follows. *Skipping* is a combination of two simple locomotor patterns—a step-hop.

Little research has been conducted on the development of the hop, slide, gallop, or skip. Hopping on one foot successively is sometimes considered a type of jumping action and can be traced in children as early as 43 months. Sliding and galloping, which are both a leap-step, result in an uneven rhythmical tempo (long-short). Because of the uneven gait, they may be expected to develop somewhat later. Skipping, too, requires an uneven gait and control of the pattern on both sides of the body. As a result, the skipping pattern may be the last locomotor skill to develop. Mature patterns of hopping and skipping involve arm and leg opposition, whereas sliding and galloping involve leading with the same arm and leg. At beginning stages children may hop, slide, gallop, or skip with the dominant leg as the lead leg. Later at a mature stage they should be able to perform each skill equally well with either leg leading.

As with previously discussed locomotor concepts, children should be exposed to a variety of experiences that enable them to include hopping, sliding, galloping, and skipping in their games. They should practice each pattern while varying the speed, direction, and pathway. They should also vary the size of the steps and the amount of force they use while taking each step. Smooth movements should be contrasted with angular or jerky changes of movement.

COMBINATIONS OF MOVEMENT PATTERNS

Just as children learn to combine various locomotor patterns, they should learn to combine various manipulative patterns; then they should learn to combine the two combinations (various manipulative patterns with locomotor patterns). Prior to this point the emphasis in each of the chapters has been on learning each of the manipulative patterns separately. This approach was selected because children can initially best learn one concept at a time. At stages of specific and diversive exploration, children need a chance to vary the conditions under which they perform each concept. This enables them to progress from elementary to mature standards of performance within each concept. The development of these skills happens at a time when children are progressing from egocentric characteristics to cooperative play and when they can cognitively relate to only a few easily understood game rules and strategies. Gradually, however, children become adept at performing each of the manipulative skills at a time when they can also handle the social complexities of team play and the cognitive aspects of more definitive rules and strategies. In fact, the upper elementary and adolescent years are a time when children reach a stage of readiness in which they are physically, mentally, emotionally, and socially ready to engage in team games.

For lead-up games to the popular conventional team sports—baseball, basketball, volleyball, soccer, football, and the like—children should be encouraged to combine the locomotor and manipulative skills that they have developed in meaningful situations. In reality, baseball is a game in which the concepts of throwing, catching, striking, running, and sliding are combined. Basketball combines running, jumping, sliding (guarding), passing, shooting, dribbling, and tipping. Each game in turn may be analyzed for its combination of manipulative and locomotor skills. For purposes of this chapter, game situations will be created in which various manipulative and locomotor concepts will be combined. Rather than consider the development of the official team sports, emphasis will be placed on creating situations in which children can make decisions about combining manipulative and locomotor concepts, rules, strategies, and social interactions. Some games will inescapably be similar to the official team sports. Others, hopefully, will be original.

CARRYING ACTIVITIES THROUGH EXPLORATION AND PROBLEM SOLVING

1. While remaining in a stationary position, hold onto or maintain contact with an object without allowing it to touch the floor. Which body parts may be used to hold or carry the object?
2. Begin moving through space at a slow pace while carrying an object with different body parts. Can you change your direction of movement while carrying the object? Can you change your level while carrying the object? Vary your pathway on the floor as you carry the object.
3. Experiment carrying objects while changing your method of locomotion. Try crawling, slithering on the floor, walking, running, hopping, jumping, skipping, etc. Does your method of carrying the object vary with your type of locomotion?
4. Try nos. 2 and 3 by increasing your rate of speed. Progress from slow to fast movements within each type of locomotor skill. Remember to vary your direction and pathway as you start and stop quickly.
5. Carry objects of varying weights. Change the relationship of the object to your body by carrying it close to and far away from your body. Would you say it is easier or harder to carry heavy objects when held close to the body? Far away from the body?
6. Carry objects of varying size. As the object increases in size, how can you best carry it?

7. If an object is bigger or heavier than one person can efficiently carry, try carrying it with a partner or small group. How can your group cooperate to carry a big or heavy object?

LOCOMOTOR ACTIVITIES THROUGH EXPLORATION AND PROBLEM SOLVING*

1. Begin walking around the floor among your classmates. Change the direction in which you walk, sometimes moving forward, sideward, and backward.
2. As you continue to walk, begin to change your pathway on the floor. Walk in straight, direct pathways; curved, circular pathways; and indirect, zigzag pathways.
3. Try different ways to combine your direction and pathway as you continue to walk. Can you walk forward in a circular or zigzag pathway? Can you walk sideward in a straight or circular pathway? How many other combinations can you try?
4. Now try walking as you vary the force of your steps. Sometimes walk heavily, other times walk softly.
5. Vary the length of your steps, sometimes taking short steps and long steps.
6. Change the flow of your walk. Walk smoothly, then jerky.
7. Quicken the pace of your walk, then walk as slowly as you can.
8. Start and stop quickly as you change the direction and pathway of your walk.
9. This time try to vary the flow, speed (pace), force, and length of your walking steps. Walk fast and lightly while taking long, then short, steps. Walk slow, heavily while taking long steps. Try to combine these factors in other ways.
10. Vary the texture gradient and levels of the surface on which you walk. Walk on smooth and rough surfaces and up and down hills.
11. Combine all these factors at one time. Vary your direction, pathway, speed, force, flow, and length of your steps as you walk. Add texture gradients and levels to these factors.
12. Walk with a partner while you vary your relationship. Walk side by side. Walk near, then far away from your partner. As you meet, walk face to face, then back to back.
13. Try to perform activities 1 to 12 as you change your method of locomotion to running. Then, leap, hop, jump, gallop, slide, and skip while you attempt the activities.

---

*A separate book could be written on the development of each concept specific to locomotion. Because of the limited scope of this book, however, only selected locomotor situations that may be applied to children's games and manipulation will be discussed.

14. Perform various locomotor movements as you attempt to move through an obstacle course made with tires, chairs, hoops, ropes, mats, etc. Attempt to move over, on, under, around, through, between, and among the objects. (The objective of this experience is to make children aware of the body shapes, forces, speeds, etc. necessary for them to fit through small spaces.) Concentrate on walking, running, hopping, skipping, and other movements while using direct and indirect pathways.
15. Run, then slide at a low level at a base on a target.
16. Jump to a high level in an attempt to touch a target suspended overhead or to propel your body over an obstacle such as a rope, hurdle, or high jump bar. Try different methods of jumping or vary your jumping style.
17. Now combine locomotor movements as you circulate among your classmates. Can you take two walking steps, a hop, and a jump and repeat the sequence over and over? Can you jump three times, take three hops, and two sliding steps to the side and repeat the sequence over and over? What other combinations can you try? Keep them simple at first, then try more complex combinations.
18. As you continue to combine locomotor movements, remember to vary your direction, pathway, speed, force, flow, etc.
19. While combining locomotor experiences, develop a sequence with a partner. Concentrate on your relationship with your partner. While performing your sequence move side by side, face to face, and/or back to back. Meet or come near your partner, then part or go away from each other. You may wish to mirror your partner's actions or shadow them: one partner performs a sequence and then the other repeats it. For example, while moving side by side with a partner, you may take four hops on the left foot, then four jumps on both feet, and finally eight gallops in a forward direction. On the hopping steps you may choose to part in a diagonal line, then jump in a diagonal pathway to meet again.

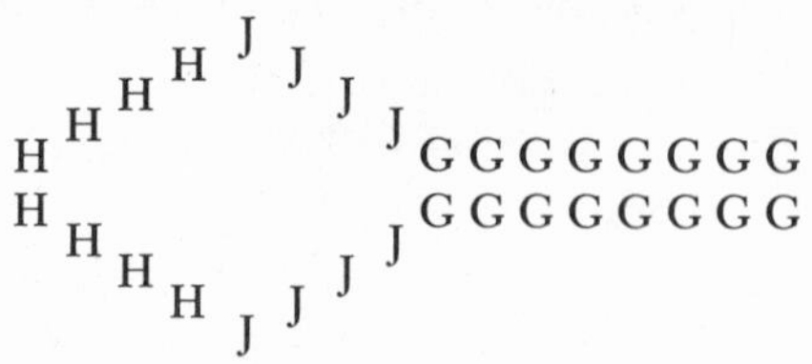

```
            J
         H     J
      H           J
   H                 J
H                      G G G G G G G G
H                      G G G G G G G G
   H                 J
      H           J
         H     J
            J
```

COMBINATION ACTIVITIES THROUGH EXPLORATION AND PROBLEM SOLVING

1. Begin by combining one locomotor skill with one manipulative skill. Vary the qualities of space, force, time, flow, and relationships as you combine these two skills. Some examples follow:
   a. Run while carrying the ball. Change your direction and pathway. Move sometimes fast, sometimes slow.

b. Hop while bouncing or dribbling the ball. Vary the force and level at which you bounce the ball. Change the leg on which you hop, the hand(s) with which you bounce the ball, and the direction and pathway of your hopping patterns.
c. Jump while throwing and catching. Jump high into the air and throw or catch the ball. Jump forward, backward, and to the side as you throw and catch the ball. Be aware of situations in which your body parts or your whole body is bent, stretched, wide, or narrow while you throw and catch during your jumps.
d. Kick and trap a ball while running. Keep the ball near your body as you dribble the ball along the ground while quickly changing your direction and pathway. Move continuously in one direction as you kick the ball while keeping it close to your body. Run and kick the ball as far as you can. Go retrieve it.

(These examples show no real progression, which is not intended at this point. The challenge is to combine one locomotor skill with one manipulative skill. The variety is endless. How many other combinations can you think of?)

2. Now begin to combine manipulative and locomotor experiences while working with a partner.
   a. While running, pass a ball back and forth with a partner. Start running side by side while close together. Move in a straight pathway. How much force do you use when passing a ball close to your partner? Now pass the ball while moving farther apart. Change your pathways to circular or zigzag. Change your speeds. Instead of moving side by side, meet and part as you pass the ball.
   b. Kick and trap a ball while running on a field with a partner. Perform the same activities as in no. 2a.
   c. Jump into the air and throw or strike a ball to a partner. Begin the experience while both of you are in a stationary position and a reasonable distance apart. Then, one or both of you may begin to move around. You may also try to catch a thrown or struck ball while in the air after a jump.
   d. While using a racket and a ball or shuttlecock, strike the object back and forth with a partner. Concentrate on running to the object and striking it back to your partner under control. Sometimes make your partner move forward, backward, and sideward as he runs, hops, slides, etc. to meet the object and strike it.

(Again, these examples show no progression, nor are they all-inclusive. The challenge is to select movement concepts to be combined and have children cooperate with a partner to execute the skill while on the move. Combine other manipulative and locomotor experiences as they fit your needs for game implementation.)

3. To this point you have been combining one locomotor skill with one manipulative skill, with and without a partner. Now experiment with a variety of ways to combine locomotor and manipulative skills while moving or advancing a ball on a field of play. For example, you could throw and catch (pass), shoot, dribble, rebound, and tip a ball while running, jumping, and sliding. You may also run and jump while carrying, passing, kicking, and trapping. Concentrate on starting, stopping, changing directions, and changing speeds while manipulating the ball.
4. Finally, combine various locomotor and manipulative skills while working with a partner against one or more opponents. Players on offense should concentrate on moving with or without the ball. Move to open spaces. Cut and use direct and indirect pathways through narrow holes or paths that lead toward a goal. Players on defense should try to guard offensive players, protect the goal, and close pathways toward the goal that may be open.

GUIDED DISCOVERY PROBLEMS FOR CARRYING

1. Can you carry an object while you are moving, stopping, starting, and changing directions and pathways? What parts of your body can you use to carry the object? (You may carry the object under your chin, in your armpit, between your knees, or in one or both hands.) Which parts work best? Why? (The hands work best because they are designed for the most effective manipulation of objects.)
2. Can you change hands and carry the object on different sides of the body as you move downfield? Why might you want to change sides while carrying an object? (Because you might want to protect the object from an opponent or prepare to pass or hand the object to another player.)
3. If someone is guarding you and you want to protect the ball from your opponent, how can you best carry it? (In both hands close to your body or in the hand opposite the side being guarded by your opponent.) Why? (The idea is to protect the ball from your opponent as much as possible.)
4. Do nos. 1 to 3 apply when you are carrying an object with an implement (lacrosse stick [scoop], etc.)? (Yes.)
5. What are some ways you can carry and then pass an object (baton or ball) to a teammate while you are both moving in the same direction or in opposite directions? The objective is to maintain continuous contact with the object without losing control. What types of handoffs work best while running slowly? While running fast? What are some ways to use blind and open passes when you are moving with a teammate in the same direction? Under what conditions can you pass from right to right, left to left, right to left, left to right, or both to both?
6. Can you carry an object and then lateral it to someone else while moving

down a field of play? Why might you choose to carry and then pass the object to a teammate during a game? (You can carry the object while no one is guarding you and pass it to someone else when you are guarded closely. In general, you pass to someone who has moved to an open area.)

7. When attempting to lift and carry a heavy object, what are some factors to consider? (When lifting a load that one person can manage, keep a straight back and lift with the legs. When carrying the load, hold it close to the body in line with the base of support. An object that is too heavy for one person should be carried cooperatively by two or more or be put on an inclined plane, pulley, and/or wheel (dolly or transporter) system for transportation.)

GUIDED DISCOVERY PROBLEMS FOR LOCOMOTOR ACTIVITIES

1. The feet can be used in five different ways for weight transfer as you perform various locomotor movements through space. Experiment with different types of stepping actions and see if you can discover what the five types of weight transfer are. (One foot to the opposite, one foot to the same, two feet to two feet, two feet to one foot, and one foot to two feet.) (See Fig. 5-2.)
2. When you transfer your weight from one foot to the other as you move through space, what are you doing? (Walking, running, or leaping.) What

Fig. 5-2. Different types of weight transfer are used in hopscotch games.

are the differences between each of these three movements? Are your arms moving in opposition to your legs in each of these skills? Do you move your arms in a forward-backward motion or across the front of your body as you perform each of these skills? Compare the rate of speed (pace), length of stride, and length of flight phase for each of these movements. How do you use your trunk and arms for increased momentum and balance in each of these skills?

3. What is it called when you transfer your weight from one foot to the same foot? (Hopping.) Can you hop first on one foot several times, then on the opposite? Do you bend at the knee, ankle, and hip after each hop to absorb your body's force? Do you use your arms to aid in your balance and help initiate the hopping motion?
4. The remaining forms of weight transfer are classified as jumping actions. Can you remember the three remaining types of weight transfer? (Two feet to two feet, one foot to two feet, and two feet to one foot.) How do you coordinate the action of your arms to aid in your jumping action? Do you establish a body lean in the direction of each jump? Can you effectively take off and land on one foot and two feet?
5. See if you can combine two or more of the five weight transfers into a sequence of four movements. What combinations can you develop? (Walk, walk, walk, hop; hop, hop, hop, jump; etc. The variety is endless.) How many can you create? Can you repeat your sequences?
6. Now combine two of the five weight transfers into a sequence that you can repeat over and over. What are some of your solutions? (Walk, hop; leap, step; and hop, jump.) Are any of these sequences given special names? (Yes. A walk-hop is a skip. A leap-step is either sliding or galloping.)
7. If you want to start running or moving fast in one direction, what can you do with your arms, legs, and body to help initiate your motion? (Lean in the direction of your intended movement and pump your arms vigorously in opposition to the action of your legs.)
8. What are some factors to consider when running efficiently? (That depends on the type of running you are doing. When jogging, land on the back of the foot and push off on the ball of the foot. When sprinting, use more of the front of the foot for takeoff and landing. High knee action to allow the lower leg to swing through is important in all types of running. The arms should swing in a forward-backward arc rather than across the midline of the body. The greater the speed of the run, the greater the body lean.)
9. How can you stop effectively, especially after moving at a fast rate of speed? (Take short, choppy steps and lean somewhat backward by bending at the knees and hips.)
10. Run an obstacle course, shuttle run, or traffic cone maze. What are some

techniques you can use to start, stop, and change directions quickly as you progress from start to finish?

11. How can you use your arms and body most effectively to perform hopping and jumping actions? (The arms may be swung up and/or out to establish momentum for the locomotor skill. The trunk of the body may lean in the direction of movement and be fully extended to achieve height and/or distance.)
12. How can you use your body effectively to land softly and efficiently from a jump or another locomotor movement? (Bend at the hips, knees, and ankles to absorb the force from the body's momentum.)
13. Some games require a specific number of steps to be taken before an event is performed (running, long jump, high jump, javelin, and bowling approach). Can you find a line or mark and take 47, 11, 20, 30 or more steps (walking or running) to reach it? Start slowly and build up your body's momentum to a peak as you reach your mark. Your last step should touch the mark.
14. Use a rope, tire, or stick as a high jump barrier. What are some ways you can get over the barrier? Try one- and two-foot takeoffs and one- and two-foot landings. Sometimes land and roll. Try using a scissors or flop style as you go over the barrier. What is the best way to get over the barrier?

GUIDED DISCOVERY PROBLEMS FOR COMBINATION ACTIVITIES

1. What are some ways you can move an object down a field of play during a game situation? (You have many choices, depending on the rules of the game. You can carry the ball while running. You can bounce or kick the ball while running. You can also choose to throw, strike, pass, or kick the ball to a teammate while in a stationary position or while on the move.) Under what conditions might you perform each of these skills? Illustrate some games in which these combined skills are implemented.
2. Play with a partner to practice throwing and catching the ball while on the move. As the thrower, what must you do to throw the ball to your partner? (Anticipate and throw a lead pass.) As a catcher, what can you do to catch a ball while on the move? (Be ready to catch the ball with your hands at any level and in any position to the front or side of your body.)
3. Play with a partner to practice kicking and trapping the ball while on the move. As the kicker, what must you do to kick the ball to your partner? (Anticipate and kick a lead pass.) As the trapper, what can you do to receive and control the ball? (Be ready to absorb the force of the ball with either leg or another body part, depending on the level of the ball and the speed with which it is traveling.)
4. Can you jump high into the air and throw and catch the ball at the peak of

your jump? What must you do? In what games might this skill be implemented?

5. Can you jump high into the air and strike the ball at the peak of your jump? What must you do? In what games might this skill be implemented?
6. Play with a partner to practice striking an object with or without an implement while on the move. What is the proper body alignment for striking the ball? Do you perform any special sliding or hopping steps when preparing to strike the ball? After striking the ball, is there anything you do to prepare to hit the ball again? (Yes, return to the center of the playing area and assume a ready position so that you may move in any direction for another return.)
7. Name some games and identify situations in which two or more skills are combined at the same time. After a brief discussion, practice these combinations under gamelike conditions.

COOPERATIVE AND COMPETITIVE GAMES

The remainder of this chapter is intended to develop several model themes, or focuses, around which children may organize their games experiences. The following game themes will focus on the processes of carrying objects, locomotion, and the combination of locomotor and manipulative experiences. It is your role as teacher to help children learn about and play within the framework, or guidelines, for game playing, as outlined in Chapter 1. After the children have become familiar with various playing areas, field designs, open and closed games, time factors, scoring systems, strategies, penalties for rule infractions, etc., they may design their own games according to their own level of abilities and interests. Initial games tend to be cooperative in nature with a few simple rules. Later the games will involve more rules, a higher level of strategy, and competition.

■ Given a box, piece of apparatus, or object of varying weight, size, and shape, make up a game that involves carrying as the primary focus, or theme. Use one or more of the following rules as a subtheme of your game.

Rules

1. Carry the object with various parts of your body: on your back, in your hand, change hands, both hands, in your arm(s), between your legs, in your mouth, etc.
2. Use an implement to carry your objects. For example, place a ball in a scoop, a peanut in a spoon, a ball in a lacrosse stick, a ball in a towel.
3. Vary your pathway, sometimes being direct while moving in straight lines and at other times being indirect while moving in zigzag or curved lines.
4. Cooperate with a partner or small group by carrying an object together.

5. Place a premium on speed by seeing who can perform the carrying task the fastest.
6. Carry the object at various levels—low, medium, and high.
7. Carry the object over, under, around, through, between, in, out, up, and down as you move through space.
8. Change distances as you perform tasks—carry objects short and long distances.
9. Working with a partner or a small group, take turns carrying each other. Be careful to develop a trusting relationship so as not to drop someone at the expense of winning a race.

■ Given a hard-surface area, make up a locomotor game with your partners (group of 2 to 6 players) in which you use at least three of the five weight transfers. Use one or more of the following rules as the focus of your game.

Rules

1. Step, hop, or jump into various boxes in the number or alphabet grid (p. 45). Concentrate on stepping, hopping, or jumping in different directions. Make long and short locomotor efforts.
2. Step, hop, or jump into various states as you combine locomotor actions on a map grid.
   a. Identify the state as you land in it.
   b. Name the capital.
   c. Tell something about the state—nickname, major products, state bird, etc.
3. Design a new type of hopscotch pattern on the ground and play with a friend.

■ Given benches, ropes, hoops, chairs, mats, and various pieces of gymnastic equipment, make up a game with your partners that focuses on locomotor skills. Use one or more of the following rules as the focus of your game. (See Fig. 5-3.)

Rules

1. Concentrate on changing your body level as you move from one piece of equipment to another.
2. Allow for changes of direction as you move along or from one piece of apparatus to another.
3. Create opportunities in which you may go over, under, around, through, and between pieces of equipment.
4. Change speeds as you move along the apparatus.
5. Use various body parts for purposes of locomotion on the apparatus—hands and knees, arms and belly, hands and feet, etc.
6. Work on relationships as you move near or far away from another player. Sometimes try to get close without touching, and sometimes move far apart.

Fig. 5-3. Use locomotor skills to move around the apparatus.

7. Mirror your partners' actions as you move on the same or different pieces of equipment.
8. Make up a game of follow-the-leader on the equipment.
9. Make up a tag game as you move on the equipment.

■ Given a long or short jump rope, develop some rope activities that you and a small group of children can perform while concentrating on the five different types of weight transfer. Use one or more of the following rules as the focus of your game.

Rules

1. Jump the rope in forward and backward directions.
2. Jump the rope while it is turned slowly, then fast.
3. Develop a variety of tricks while jumping a short rope.
   a. Vary the five weight transfers while jumping.
   b. Hop or skip while turning the rope.
   c. Do a double turnaround on one jump.
   d. Cross arms while jumping forward and backward.
4. Jump a short rope while jumping a long rope turned by others at the same time.
5. Develop a variety of tricks while jumping a long rope.
   a. Turn around.
   b. Touch your knees, feet, the floor, etc.
   c. Clap your hands.

Fig. 5-4. Jump rope with a partner.

   d. Bounce a ball.
   e. Twirl a Hula-Hoop.
6. Jump with a partner while side by side, face to face, back to back, front to back. (See Fig. 5-4.)
7. Make up a jump rope rhyme to which you can jump rhythmically.
8. Make up a sequence of steps with which you can jump to music. Use some of the latest popular hits and make up a jump rope routine.

■ Given a rectangular, circular, or open space or space with a variety of obstacles, make up a game with a small group of children that places a premium on running and tagging or chasing and fleeing. Use one or more of the following rules as the focus of your game.

Rules

1. Emphasize direct locomotor pathways such as running straight from one point to another.
2. Emphasize also indirect locomotor pathways such as starting, stopping, and changing directions quickly.
3. Vary the type of locomotor pattern used—walk, run, hop, skip, etc.
4. Allow for changes of speed in your game—slow, fast.
5. Stress cooperation in your game. For example, hold hands and move with a partner while trying to catch others in your game.
6. Start your game with one member being it; as others are caught, have them help to catch the remaining players.
7. Have a goal or a predetermined body pose that offers a safe zone or free period from which you may not be caught. A person cannot stay in the free zone or body pose too long or too many times. For example, a person may only use the free zone three to five times or no more than 10 seconds during any one game.

8. Vary the formation of your game—line, circle, small group, scatter, etc.
9. Develop a theme for your game and some word cues:
   a. Hunt—players may be different animals.
   b. Space—goals or locations and distances to different planets.
   c. Streets and alleys—players move in straight lines down streets or alleys.
   d. Traffic cop—tell players when to stop and go.
10. Tag on various parts of a person's body, take a flag (Fig. 5-14) away, or tag a person with an object such as a ball.

■ Given a ball and a field of play, design a game that focuses on a combination of carrying, throwing, catching, and/or striking (with the hand) patterns. With a partner or small group, design your game to include one or more of the following rules.

Rules

1. Include various locomotor skills in your game—run, hop, jump, slide, etc.
   a. Change your direction as you move.
   b. Change your floor pathways as you move.
   c. Change your speed as you move.
   d. Change your relationship to your partner or small group as you play your game—face to face, side by side, circle, scatter, etc.
2. Vary the force of your manipulative actions as you move near or farther away from other players or a target area.
3. As you manipulate the ball in different ways and styles, change the level of your actions—high, medium, and low.
4. Choose a specific direction in which you wish to project the ball—up, down, or out away from your body.
5. When you perform various throwing, catching, and/or striking actions, you may wish to develop rules as to how many times the ball is allowed to touch the ground under varying conditions—0, 1, 2, 3, or unlimited.
6. If your game has boundaries, you may wish to make a rule about what happens if a ball goes out-of-bounds.
7. If your game includes carrying, throwing, catching, and/or striking, you may wish to specify a number of steps or time period after which the ball must be exchanged.
8. Move the ball to a designated person, area, or target, at which time a goal may be scored. You may or may not want to keep track of your score. You may also wish to specify a number of attempts at scoring a goal—1, 2, 3, or unlimited.
9. Concentrate on working cooperatively with a partner or small group for a common goal or compete against your partner or another group as you play your game.

■ Given a ball and any implement, develop a net- or field-oriented game that focuses on a combination of carrying, throwing, catching, and/or striking (with the implement) patterns. With a partner or small group, design your game to include one or more of the following rules.

Rules

1. Include various locomotor skills in your game—run, hop, jump, slide, etc. and at the same time:
   a. Allow for changes of direction as you move.
   b. Allow for changes of floor pathway as you move.
   c. Allow for changes in speed as you move.
   d. Change your relationship with your partner or small group as you play your game—face to face, side by side, circle, line, scatter, etc.
   e. Practice moving with and without the ball.
   f. Practice moving on offense and defense.
2. Vary the force of your manipulative actions as you move near or far away from other players or a target area.
3. As you manipulate the ball in different ways and styles, change the level of your actions—high, medium, and low.
4. Choose a specific direction in which you wish to project the ball—up, down, or out away from your body.
5. As you carry, throw, catch, and/or strike the ball with an implement, you may wish to develop rules as to how many times the ball is allowed to touch the ground under varying conditions—0, 1, 2, 3, or unlimited.
6. If your game has boundaries, you may wish to make a rule about what happens if a ball goes out-of-bounds.
7. If your game includes carrying, throwing, catching, and/or striking with an implement, you may wish to specify a number of steps or a time period after which the ball must be exchanged.
8. Move the ball to a designated person, area, or target, at which time a goal may be scored. You may or may not want to keep track of your score. You may also wish to specify a number of attempts at scoring a goal—1, 2, 3, or unlimited.
9. Concentrate on working cooperatively with a partner or small group for a common goal or compete against your partner or another group as you play your game.

■ Given a ball and a field of play, design a game that focuses on a combination of carrying, throwing, catching, kicking, and/or trapping patterns. With a partner or small group, design your game to include one or more of the following rules.

Rules

1. Include various locomotor skills in your game—run, jump, slide, etc. and at the same time:
   a. Allow for changes of direction as you move.

   b. Allow for changes of floor pathway as you move.
   c. Allow for changes in speed as you move.
   d. Change your relationship with your partner or small group as you play your game—face to face, side by side, near, far, line, scatter, etc.
   e. Practice moving with and without the ball.
   f. Practice moving on offense and defense.
2. Vary the force of your manipulative actions as you move near or far away from other players or a target area.
3. As you manipulate the ball in different ways and styles, change the level of your actions—high, medium, and low.
4. Choose a specific direction in which you wish to project the ball—up, down, or out away from your body.
5. As you carry, throw, catch, kick and/or trap the ball, you may wish to develop rules as to how many times the ball is allowed to touch the ground under varying conditions—0, 1, 2, 3, or unlimited.
6. If your game has boundaries, you may wish to make a rule about what happens if a ball goes out of bounds.
7. If your game includes carrying, throwing, catching, kicking, and/or trapping, you may wish to specify a number of steps or time period after which the ball must be exchanged.
8. Move the ball to a designated person, area or target, at which time a goal may be scored. You may also wish to specify a number of attempts at scoring a goal—1, 2, 3, or unlimited.
9. Concentrate on working cooperatively with a partner or small group for a common goal or compete against your partner or another group as you play your game.

SAMPLE GAMES

GAME 1

Major focus: With a partner or small group, cooperatively carry someone to safety.

Number of players: 2 to 20.

Equipment: An obstacle course made from hoops, ropes, tires, jungle gym, balance beam, slide, tables, etc.

Playing area: Any indoor or outdoor playing area on which an obstacle course may be set up (Fig. 5-5).

Rules: The intention of this game is to create an atmosphere of trust and cooperation through an adventure or challenge experience. The children are to pretend they are on a rock-climbing or backpacking trip and someone gets hurt. They must then find a way to carry that person to safety. The children may want to carry the injured person themselves or use a type of stretcher. They may even want to splint a leg, arm, etc. to make the experience more realistic. The game can challenge the children to carry the "injured" person over a distance within a time limit (before dark); a long distance; or over, under, and through various obstacles.

Fig. 5-5. Carry your partner to safety.

GAME 2

Major focus: Carry an object over direct and indirect pathways in an attempt to cross the playing area without dropping the object.

Number of players: 20 to 30.

Equipment: 10 to 15 balls.

Playing area: A rectangular area 30 × 60 or 50 × 80 feet (Fig. 5-6).

Rules: Players are divided into two teams of equal size. Those on offense are each given a ball to carry. The objective is to see how many times they can cross the playing area without dropping the ball they are carrying in a given time limit (1 to 3 minutes). Specific contests can be to carry the ball in the right hand only, left hand only, or both hands. Players on defense may pivot as if one foot is nailed to the floor while trying to slap or knock the ball out of the hands of the offensive players. The playing area should be restricted to make conditions somewhat crowded. Precautions should be taken to have defensive players aim at the ball and not just hack at offensive players' arms and bodies. After the given time limit, offensive and defensive teams trade roles.

Scoring: Scoring may be as individuals or by team. One point is scored for each successful crossing without dropping the ball. As a result, individuals may keep their own score, or scores may be added for a team score.

Fig. 5-6. Avoid dropping the ball when crossing the playing area.

GAME 3

Major focus: Children learn to make decisions quickly and chase or evade a partner by moving in direct pathways.

Number of players: 2 to 30.

Equipment: None.

Playing area: An open space, for purposes of locomotor movement, approximately 40 × 80 feet (Fig. 5-7).

Rules: This game may be played with two or more sets of partners. Players stand across from their partner at a midline in the play area. Each set of partners begins the game by saying "Rock, paper, scissors" or "1, 2, 3" while shaking their hand up and down three times. After the three count sequence, partners simultaneously make a sign with the hand they were shaking. Children have a choice of three signs. A fist means rock. A flat, extended hand means paper. A fist with index and middle fingers extended means scissors. After each sequence partners compare signs. A paper covers rock. A rock breaks scissors. A scissors cuts paper. Sequentially the paper, rock, and scissors are dominant factors. When children choose the same sign, they neutralize each other. After each shaking sequence the player with the dominant sign must chase the partner to the end line. The person with the subdominant sign must react quickly and flee to the end line and avoid being tagged. When neutral signs are given, both players remain still.

Scoring: The game may be scored individually or as a cumulative team score. After each shake and ensuing chase, a player or team may score a point under the following conditions:

1. Neutral signs—0 points.
2. Subdominant sign evades freely to end line—0 points.
3. Dominant sign catches evader before end line—1 point.

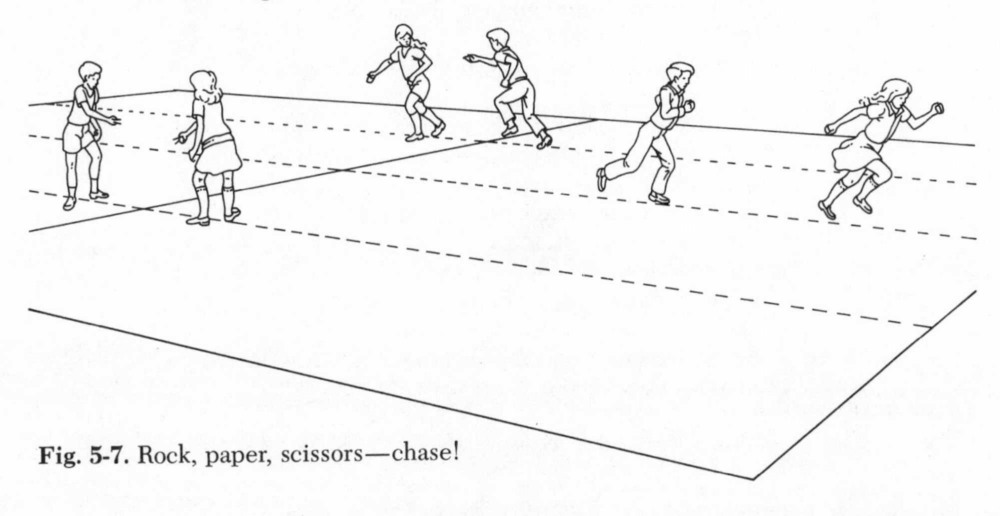

Fig. 5-7. Rock, paper, scissors—chase!

GAME 4

Major focus: Work cooperatively with a group in an effort to vary and improve the five basic weight transfers as forms of locomotion and to stimulate creativity and interaction among group members.

Number of players: 3 or more.

Equipment: One long jump rope for each group of 3 children.

Playing area: Any open flat surface, indoors or outdoors (Fig. 5-8).

Rules: The purpose of this lesson is to vary and improve the five basic weight transfers by jumping rope. While jumping rope, the children should jump from one foot to the same, one to the other, two to two, two to one, and one to two. They should jump fast and slow with and without a rebound. They should change body shapes, levels, directions, and relationships with the turners as they jump. Practicing to go in the front and back door should also be a part of the experience. To make the activity more gamelike, the children should be encouraged to chant jump rope rhymes and perform various tasks while jumping. Two examples follow:

Teddie Bear, Teddie Bear,
Turn around (*jumper turns around*);
Teddie Bear, Teddie Bear,
Touch the ground (*jumper touches ground with hand*);
Teddie Bear, Teddie Bear,
Clap your hands (*jumper claps hands*);
Teddie Bear, Teddie Bear,
Parade and prance (*jumper lifts knees high*);
Teddie Bear, Teddie Bear,
Go upstairs (*jumper moves toward head of rope*);
Teddie Bear, Teddie Bear,
Say your prayers (*jumper folds hands*);
Teddie Bear, Teddie Bear,
Turn out the light (*jumper reaches overhead*);
Teddie Bear, Teddie Bear,
Say good night (*jumper closes eyes*);

Not last night, but the night before
Twenty-four robbers came knocking at my door.
I ran out and they ran in,
And this is the song they sang to me:
Spanish dancer, do a split;
Spanish dancer, do a high kick;
Spanish dancer, turn around;
Spanish dancer, touch the ground;
Spanish dancer, do the kangaroo (*squat and jump*);
Spanish dancer, skit, skat, skidoo!

The children should be encouraged to work cooperatively and take turns. Ample time should be provided to vary the chants by creating additional rhymes and new stunts. Ultimately the children should be encouraged to make up their own original rhymes, chants, and jumping sequences. Allow them to be creative. It will not be a disappointment.

Fig. 5-8. Jump rope to chants or rhymes.

GAME 5

Major focus: Use different types of weight transfer to move from one letter to another in an attempt to spell words.
Number of players: 2 to 4.
Equipment: A piece of chalk or a can of paint and a brush.
Playing area: A 6 × 6 foot square grid on a hard-surface area. In the 1-foot boxes, 9-inch small letters of the alphabet are painted or drawn into each box. (See Fig. 5-9.)
Rules: The objective of this game is for children to combine their knowledge of spelling with their ability to perform weight transfer activities. Players work in pairs or in groups of 3. One player thinks of a word three or more letters in length. The partner or coplayer must move on the grid to spell the word, performing three or more of the five basic weight transfers (one foot to the same, one to the other, two to two, one to two, or two to one) to move sequentially from one letter to the next. On spelling the word correctly, the player may choose a word for the partner to spell. If the word is spelled incorrectly, a player must repeat the experience by sequentially spelling another word.
Scoring: No score or 1 point for each word spelled correctly.
Variations

1. Use capital letters instead of small letters.
2. Use numbers instead of letters and solve arithmetic problems by weight transfer sequences instead of spelling words.

Fig. 5-9. Spell the word by hopping into the squares.

GAME 6

Major focus: Run or use other locomotor skills over indirect pathways to avoid being tagged, or caught.

Number of players: 20 to 30.

Equipment: None.

Playing area: A rectangular area approximately 40 × 60 feet (Fig. 5-10).

Rules: The class is divided into two teams. One team goes to the middle and spreads out in scatter formation (not rows or columns). They should not be able to touch one another as they reach about in their personal space. They pretend that one foot is nailed to the ground and pivot around in their personal space, trying to catch those players attempting to cross to the opposite side (the goal). Members of the second team may try at will to cross to the opposite side untouched. If they get tagged, they may finish their journey to the opposite side by walking. They will try to cross from one side to the other and back again at will during a time period of from 1 to 5 minutes. After the time limit is up, teams exchange roles.

Scoring: Scoring may be as individuals or by team. One point is scored for each successful crossing without being touched. As a result, individuals may keep their own score, or scores may be added for a team score. In the latter event, players may strategically attract attention and get caught to allow others to cross, thereby helping the overall team score.

Fig. 5-10. Run through the playing area without getting caught.

GAME 7

Major focus: Move the ball down a field of play by combining passing (throwing and catching) and dribbling (striking) in an attempt to score a goal by throwing at a target (shooting). Work cooperatively with teammates to develop strategies to effectively move with and without the ball while being guarded by defensive players.

Number of players: 5.

Equipment: A playground ball or basketball.

Playing area: A rectangular area approximately 60 × 80 feet. Each end must have a target such as a basket, geometrical shape, tire, Hula-Hoop, or box placed at an appropriate height in a horizontal or vertical plane. (See Fig. 5-11.)

Rules: The children take turns playing three offensive players against two defensive ones. The objective is for the offensive players to dribble or pass the ball to each other while running and dodging in an attempt to move the ball down the field of play. The idea is to dribble the ball when not guarded and to pass it to an open player when being guarded. Players may not run with the ball (carrying) unless it is being dribbled. As offensive players approach the goal, the player with the best opportunity and position may throw the ball at the target (basketball goal, hoop, box, tire, or geometrical shape). The objectives of the defensive players are to guard the offensive players, intercept in the passing lanes, and prevent a goal from being scored. After each offensive set, 1 player rotates off offense and onto defense so that for every five turns there are 3 players on offense and 2 on defense.

Scoring: One point is scored for each successful attempt at making a goal. An unsuccessful attempt at a goal, such as a pass interception, the ball going out-of-bounds, traveling while carrying the ball, or a missed shot at the target, results in no score. Each successful attempt at a goal results in a point for each offensive player for that set. Players keep their own score because 1 player rotates after each offensive set.

Fig. 5-11. Pass the ball to an open player and make a basket.

GAME 8

Major focus: Strike the ball on the ground or through the air into a field of play in an effort to score a run. Catch balls rolling or bouncing on the ground or flying through the air, and throw the ball to other players in an attempt to make an out. Work cooperatively with teammates to develop strategies to score runs while on offense and to effectively defend one's territory while playing in the field.

Number of players: 14—7 per team, two teams.

Equipment: A ball, a bat, and some gloves.

Playing area: A softball diamond (Fig. 5-12).

Rules: During this game the basic rules of softball are used with several modifications. A batting tee is permitted. The 7 players in the field play the three outfield and four infield positions. The batting team supplies the catcher. A batter may take up to five swings to hit the ball in fair territory past the pitcher's mound. Outs are made the same as in softball: a fly ball caught is an out; a ground ball caught must be thrown to first base before the runner reaches the base; if a runner occupies one base, force-outs may occur at advancing bases. An inning consists of all 7 players taking a turn at bat. Teams alternate being at bat and being in the field. After each new inning, players take a new position in the field. Batting order also changes with each inning. A game consists of 5 innings.

Scoring: One run is scored as a player completes the base path, moving from first to second, third, and home base. The score for a given inning is the number of players reaching home base before seven outs are made.

Variation: If a pitcher is desired, the batting team may supply one. Again, a batter must be allowed to strike the ball into the fair territory.

Fig. 5-12. Modified softball games include a combination of locomotor and manipulative skills.

GAME 9

Major focus: Use skills of kicking and heading to propel a ball to a teammate or over a net in an attempt to score a point.

Number of players: 6—3 per team, two teams.

Equipment: One beach ball or large balloon per game and a net or rope to serve as a barrier.

Playing area: A rectangular area the size of a badminton court.

Rules: This game is designed to be an adaptation of the Taiwanese game of sepek tacraw. The rules are a combination of the games of badminton, volleyball, and soccer. A badminton court with a net is used as the playing area. The service and contact rules from the game of volleyball are applied. The te..m serving must serve from the right side of the end line. When the defensive team wins a play transaction, the players receive a side out. Players rotate after each side out so that they take turns playing each court position. The ball may be played up to three times on one side of the net before it must pass over the net. No one player may touch the ball two times in a row. The rules of soccer apply in that the ball must be kicked or headed to a teammate or over the net. To make this game feasible for upper elementary school children, the flight of the ball must be slowed considerably. To accomplish this, a beach ball or large circular balloon should be used.

Scoring: Only the serving team may score a point. Each game is played to 15 points. One point is scored by the serving team when—

1. The ball touches the floor inside the defensive team's court.
2. The ball is contacted four times by the defensive team.
3. The defensive team kicks the ball out-of-bounds on any return.

A side out is awarded the defensive team when—

1. Any one of these infractions is committed by the offensive team.

Fig. 5-13. Kick or head the beach ball over the net.

GAME 10

Major focus: Move the ball downfield by carrying, passing, and/or kicking it into or over a goal. Cooperate effectively with teammates to move a ball downfield against an opponent.

Number of players: 6 to 8.

Equipment: A football, rugby ball, or soccer ball and two flags for each player.

Playing area: A rectangular playing area approximately 20 × 40 yards with a goal on each end. The field is divided into four equal segments. (See Fig. 5-14.)

Rules: This game is a modified flag football game with 3 or 4 players per team. Each player carries a flag.

One player may function as a hiker and blocker, another as a blocker and pass receiver, and a third player as the runner and passer. Players should take turns with each role. Defensive players position themselves strategically to stop a run or a pass. The offensive team has four plays to advance the ball into the next segment or across the goal area. A play is ended when the flag is pulled from the runner's belt, when there is an incomplete pass, or when the ball or runner goes out-of-bounds. If after four plays the offensive team has not advanced the ball into the next segment or across the goal, one of them must kick (punt) the ball to the opposite team. If after four plays or less the ball is advanced into a new segment, the team in possession may start a new series of plays to move the ball into the next segment or across the goal. The game is started by a flip of the coin, the losing team kicking the ball to the winner of the flip. After each score, the scoring team must kick the ball to the opposite team. Each initial kick is made at the dividing line between the first and second segment.

Scoring: Two points are awarded each time a team moves the ball into a new segment. Four points are awarded for crossing the goal on a running play. Five points are awarded for crossing the goal on a passing play.

Fig. 5-14. Move the ball downfield to score a goal.

Bibliography

AAHPER: Youth sports guide, Washington, D.C., 1977, The Association.

Blake, O. W., and Volp, A. M. Lead-up games to team sports, Englewood Cliffs, N.J., 1964, Prentice-Hall, Inc.

Bloom, B. S., et al.: Taxonomy of educational objectives: handbook 1, the cognitive domain, New York, 1956, David McKay Co., Inc.

Browne, E.: An ethological theory of play, JOHPER **39**:36-39, Sept., 1968.

Cameron, W. McD., and Munday, S.: The games lesson, London, 1977, Cambridge University Press.

Docherty, D., and Peak, L.: Creatrad: an approach to teaching games, Journal of Physical Education and Recreation **47**:20-22, April, 1976.

Ellis, M. J.: Why people play, Englewood Cliffs, N.J., 1973, Prentice-Hall, Inc.

Ferritti, F.: The great American book of sidewalk, stoop, dirt, curb and alley games, New York, 1975, Workman Publishing Co., Inc.

Ferritti, F.: The great American marble book, New York, 1973, Workman Publishing Co., Inc.

Fluegelman, A., editor: The *new* games book, a New Games Foundation book, Garden City, New York, 1976, Doubleday & Co., Inc.

Gallahue, D. L., Werner, P. H., and Luedke, G. C.: A conceptual approach to moving and learning, New York, 1975, John Wiley & Sons, Inc.

Games teaching, Journal of Physical Education and Recreation **48**:17-35, Sept., 1977.

Gilliom, B. C.: Basic movement education for children, Reading, Mass., 1970, Addison-Wesley Publishing Co., Inc.

Johnson, S. E. D.: Frisbee, New York, 1975, Workman Publishing Co., Inc.

Learning how to play, Quest Monograph 26, Summer, 1976.

Leonard, G.: The ultimate athlete, New York, 1975, The Viking Press.

Linford, A. G., and Jeanrenaud, C.: A behavioristic model for a four stage play theory, Second International Congress of Sports Psychology, Washington, D.C., 1968.

Logsdon, B. J., et al.: Physical education for children, Philadelphia, 1978, Lea & Febiger.

Mauldon, E., and Redfern, H. B.: Games teaching, London, 1976, Macdonald & Evans, Ltd.

McClenaghan, B. A., and Gallahue, D. L.: Fundamental movement, Philadelphia, 1978, W. B. Saunders Co.

Milberg, A.: Street games, New York, 1976, McGraw Hill Book Co.

Morris, G. S. D.: How to change the games children play, Minneapolis, 1976, Burgess Publishing Co.

Mosston, M.: Teaching physical education, Columbus, Ohio, 1966, Charles E. Merrill Books, Inc.

Neuman, E.: The elements of play, New York, 1971, MSS Information Corporation.

Orlick, T., and Botterill, C.: Every kid can win, Chicago, 1975, Nelson-Hall Co.

Orlick, T.: Winning through cooperation, Washington, D.C., 1978, Hawkins & Associates.

Riley, M.: Games and humanism, Journal of Physical Education and Recreation **46:** 46-49, Feb., 1975.

Seidel, B. L., et al.: Sports skills: a conceptual approach to meaningful movements, Dubuque, Iowa, 1975, W. C. Brown Co., Publishers.

Society of Friends Peace Committee, For the fun of it: selected cooperative games for children and adults, Nonviolence and Children Program, Philadelphia, 1976, The Society.

Sutton-Smith, B.: A descriptive account of four modes of children's play between 1 and 5, New York, 1970, Columbia University Press.

Tutko, T., and Bruns, W.: Winning is everything and other American myths, New York, 1976, Macmillan Inc.

Werner, P. H., and Simmons, R.: Inexpensive physical education equipment, Minneapolis, 1976, Burgess Publishing Co.

Wickstrom, R. L.: Fundamental motor patterns, ed. 2, Philadelphia, 1977, Lea & Febiger.

Index